I0829255

The Polk Street Review

a celebration of Noblesville, IN

2021 edition

Family Traditions: Old & New

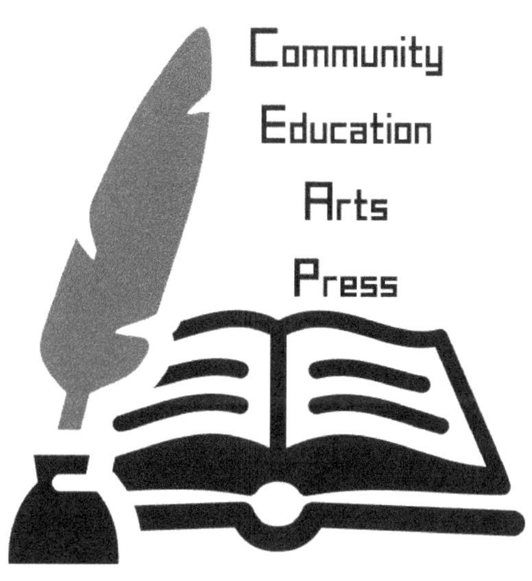

First Printing: 2021

Cover design: Alys Caviness-Gober
Cover art: *Indiana Spring* by Alys Caviness-Gober
Project design, formatting, and layout: Alys Caviness-Gober
Editors: Alys Caviness-Gober & Sarah E. Morin

ISBN: 978-0-9998858-6-4

Community • Education • Arts Press
a division of *Community • Education • Arts, Inc.*
Noblesville, IN 46060
1st Printing: February 2021
https://CEArts.org

Ordering Information:
Special discounts are available on quantity purchases by corporations, associations, educators, and others. Please contact Alys at info@cearts.org for details.
U.S. trade bookstores and wholesalers: please contact Alys at info@cearts.org for details.

Dedicated to
our community,
our friends,
and
our families

The Polk Street Review 2021 Sponsors

Community • Education • Arts (CEArts) is a 501(c)(3) nonprofit Arts organization that relies upon the support of our local community. We gratefully thank the following individuals and local businesses for their financial support of the 2021 edition of *The Polk Street Review*.

Supporters

Doug Church
Joni Corbett
Jerry Dreesen
Gal's Guide Library
Jean Roberts
Chris Stolle
Theresa Timmons
Janice Wiley

Corporate Sponsors

We're so grateful to our three corporate sponsors for their support this year, despite the economic effects of COVID-19 on businesses.

@LHOCreations tirelessly fundraised this past year and donated a portion of their Summertime Meals Service sales to our organization to help support this edition.
You can find *@LHOCreations* online at:
http://www.lhocreations.world/

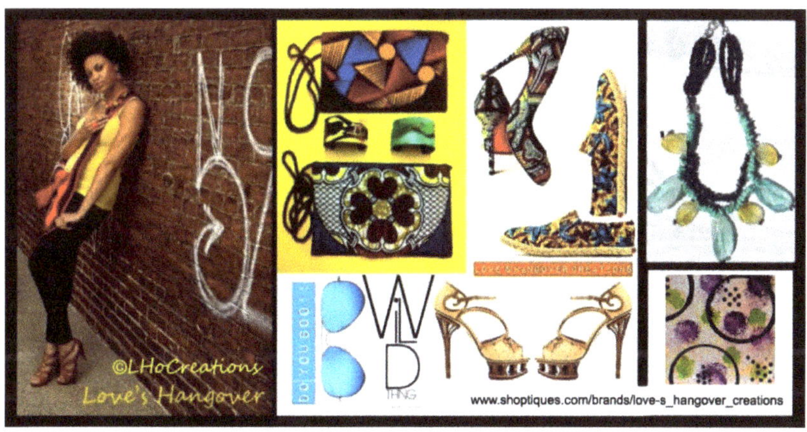

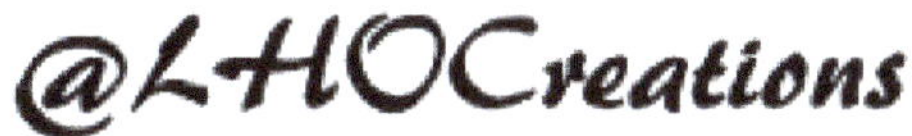

Sharpest Tool Technology Services is a user-friendly and affordable IT solutions company. It is a woman-owned small business that makes it home in Noblesville. *Sharpest Tool* again supported our publication this year, and we are so grateful for their support. We hope you will call upon *Sharpest Tool Technology Services* for your technology needs!

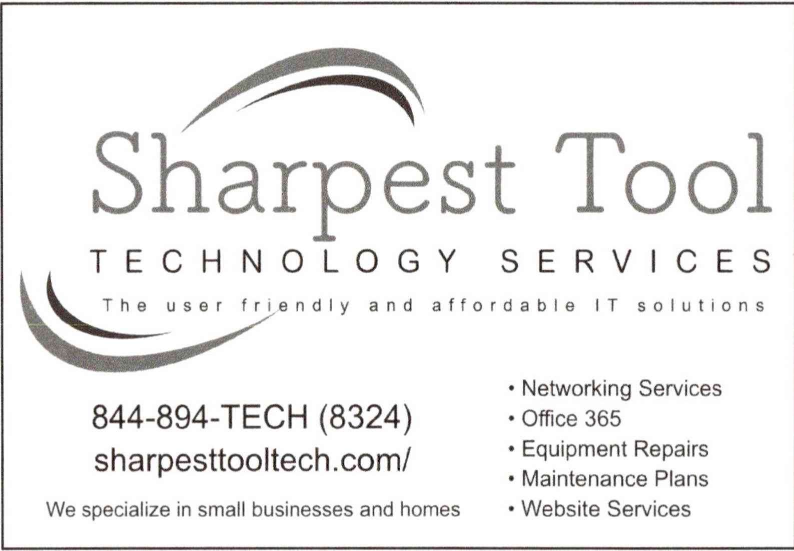

Church Church Hittle + Antrim supports the Arts in our community and we gratefully acknowledge their support for this publication of *The Polk Street Review*.

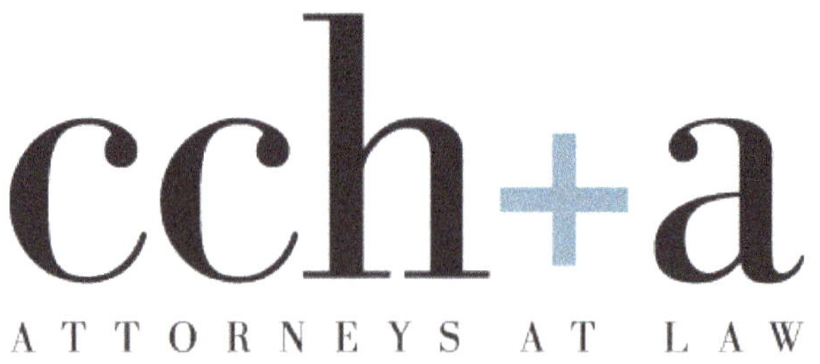

Two North Ninth Street
Noblesville, IN 46060

2021 Community • Education • Arts Acknowledgements

Community • Education • Arts, Inc. (CEArts) is a vital part of the Noblesville Cultural Arts District, and we are a paid partner to Nickel Plate Arts.

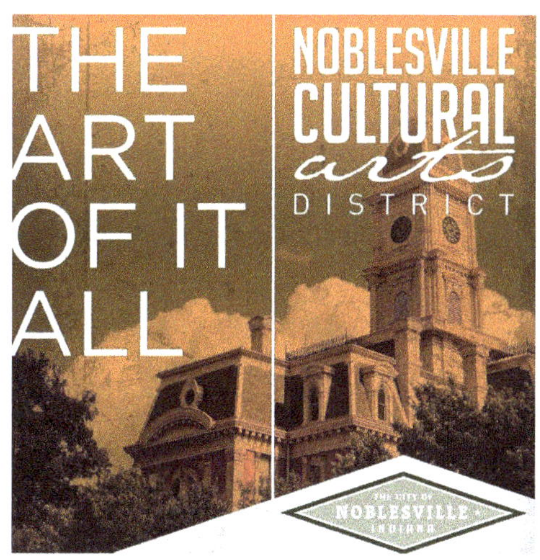

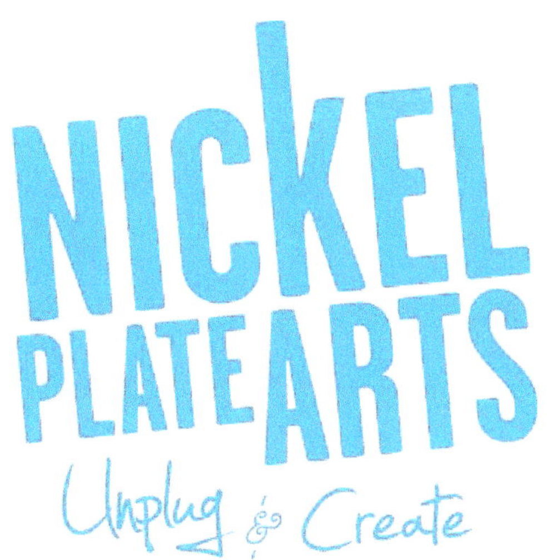

Table of Contents:

Spatial (North Alley Mural, Noblesville, IN) by Andrea Haydon

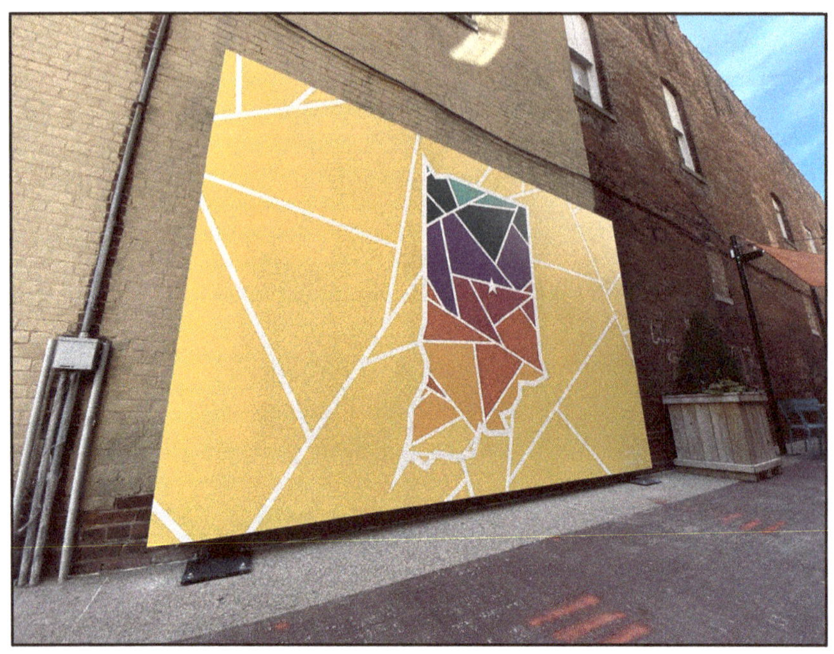

Introduction

The Polk Street Review book is named in honor of a significant historic street in Noblesville, the north/south road that had 2 historic Heritage Railway tracks running alongside and down the middle of it for 200 years. The street was named after William Conner's partner, Josiah Polk; it is now called 8th Street, and it dates back to when Noblesville was laid out in 1823. Polk Street had mills were at the north end, and the old courthouse, bars, liveries, hotels, homes, and other commercial buildings lined its southern stretch.

At some point, it became the dividing line between white-collar and blue-collar neighborhoods, white and black neighborhoods, residential and industrial areas, and high ground *versus* the flood plain. Over time those traditional divisions became so ingrained that people didn't mentioned them, but they knew them. Social and economic division are like that: they take on a life of their own unless we consciously resist them, because they become taken for granted, like history itself. Folks new to Noblesville see 8th Street as just a main route through town, but the old road represents the true history of Noblesville, her businesses, and the generations of people who have lived here.

Noblesville has seen a lot of development change; it can retain historic small-town qualities that make it unique from its neighbors, while also recognizing that certain areas, certain landmarks, and certain streets play a part in the City's vision for the future. In today's developer-driven world, we hope that Noblesville can retain a small-town feel. As we go to print with this edition of our annual anthology, amid more developments in our community, and amid a global pandemic in which Indiana ranks in the top five as a one of the "most dangerous" states to visit due to our high COVID-19 numbers, our theme this year, *Family Traditions: Old & New*, feels particularly relevant.

This is the second year we had a Theme Contest: congratulations to Vivianne Belle, who submitted the winning theme! Little did we know when we chose the winning theme back in in January 2020 that the COVID-19 global pandemic would impact our traditions so very much. We can all relate to how many of the submissions in this edition express the roller-coaster ride that has been the past year, and how hope for the future begins to glimmer more brightly as we head into the second year of the pandemic. Art as therapy is certainly something that CEArts believes in, and in the spirit of therapeutic artwork, we've opted to use a brightly-colored cover design for this edition of *The Polk Street Review*.

There are so many things we took for granted before COVID-19: the irreplaceable feeling of the small arms of our grandchildren wrapping around us in loving hugs, the joy of casual family get-togethers, congregating merrily with friends at a local art gallery or a neighborhood bar for drinks whilst listening a local singer-songwriter perform live, the easy relaxation of going out to eat, the wonder of witnessing weddings and the sorrow of saying goodbye at funerals, and so much more. Our family traditions, our community traditions, have changed, and we don't know what 2021 will look like – will we be able to go back to some of our old traditions or will we continue to adapt and embrace new ones?

Traditions are the heart of family and community; we're doing what we can, as a small nonprofit organization, to keep Noblesville's heart beating as we honor our community with this annual publication. *The Polk Street Review*'s purpose is to capture and celebrate heritage, history, and the people who live and work here (past and present!) in submissions of original prose, poetry, song lyrics, and images. Traditionally, we've asked that either the subject matter or the submitter have a connection to Noblesville. That tradition is getting harder to enforce as our organization continues to grow globally. Another TPSR tradition is using a grasshopper in our TPSR logo.

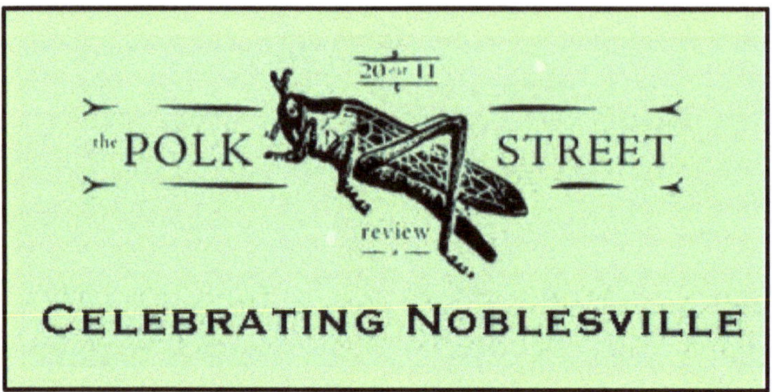

We often refer to our contributors as *grasshoppers* and to the people who quietly support them as *ants.* These insect references are taken from Aesop's fable, *The Ant & The Grasshopper*. Grasshoppers are the dreamers, the creatives: the artists, writers, and musicians among us. Ants are the ones who support them: the hardworking loved ones toiling away in the background, the ones who handle the realities of life. Grasshoppers create that which inspires, that which feeds the soul; ants create that which feeds the body. The world needs both ants and grasshoppers, so *cheers* to both!

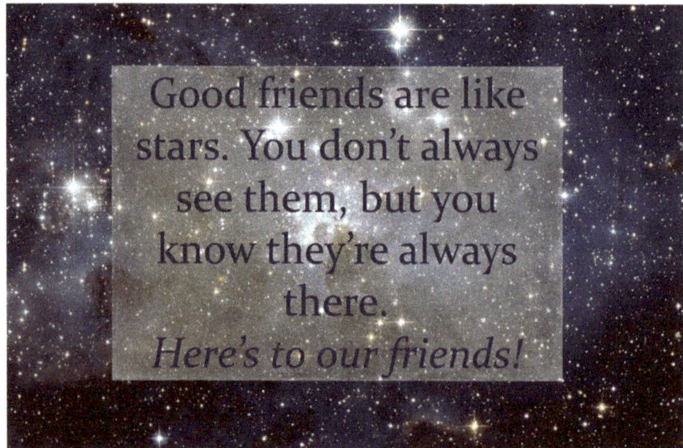

A Note from CEArts President

It is a mild pre-dawn morning in late December 2020. I'm working on the book's layout before the annual 31 December submission deadline has passed, because, like a lot of Americans, I've got some time on my hands. Due to COVID-19, since mid-March 2020 I haven't physically interacted with my friends and family, or the general public. It has been terribly hard. Words fail me to describe how much I miss my little grandson: for his first year of life, I took care of him Mon-Fri while his parents were at work. He'll be two years old in March 2021, and we haven't even hugged since his first birthday. Given my isolation, a special *thank you* goes out to my son, my daughter, my son-in-law, and my darling grandson for their willingness to Zoom with me almost daily since mid-March 2020.

I'm not alone in having pre-existing conditions that forced isolation and self-quarantine. I'm not alone in waiting for a vaccine, while knowing life won't magically be safe after getting it. The entire country needs to achieve 70% immunity before any of us will be safe without masks and social distancing. So *please*, everyone: get a vaccine as soon as you possibly can, and *please* wear a mask until we achieve that 70% nationwide.

This year I see *TPSR* as tangible proof that, despite COVID-19, creative folks are still *here*, still producing amazing art. As President of CEArts, I can't tell you how proud we are to publish the work of the creatives who submitted this year! This edition's *Family Traditions: Old & New* theme brought in wonderful pieces: poignant, hilarious, sobering, and thought-provoking reflections on the past, imaginings of the future, and good storytelling in word or image.

About the *Awards* (listed near the end of the book); no one related to anyone on the *CEArts* Board is eligible for awards, and images submitted as accompanying a written piece are not eligible for *Image* category awards. We have *First Place, Second Place, Third Place* awards in our three categories, *Prose*, *Song Lyrics & Poetry*, and *Images*. This year, the *Prose* and *Song Lyrics & Poetry* categories also have one Honorable Mention. We have two *Special Awards* this year: *Special Awards* are given in recognition of not one particular piece of writing or imagery, but rather to one or more submitters. Sometimes it is someone whose submission(s) shows us they are perhaps taking a risk (in life or art form), have a fresh perspective or voice, or we feel they warrant a special award for other reasons.

TPSR's highest honor is the *Award of Merit*, which we've nicknamed *Best in Book*. The *Award of Merit* recognizes one submission from any of the three categories that we believe will be felt deeply for a long time, in your heart and soul. Selecting the *Award of Merit* winner, and all the other awards winners, is both fun and challenging for us.

The past year has been one of unforeseen and surreal challenges for all of our *TPSR* grasshoppers and ants. It certainly was for me personally, and for our organization, and I for one am happy to embrace with joyful anticipation all of the *Family Traditions: Old & New* that will come my way in the months ahead!

I couldn't put together this book without the help, support, encouragement, and love from my ant-husband, Cris, and my grasshopper/ant-friend Sarah E. In her honor, I've placed Sarah E.'s beautiful poem, *Green Santa*, which is a tribute to her grandfather, first up in the book. After that, there's no particular order; the layout is about making everything fit on the pages. Enjoy!

Alys Caviness-Gober
President, *Community • Education • Arts, Inc.*

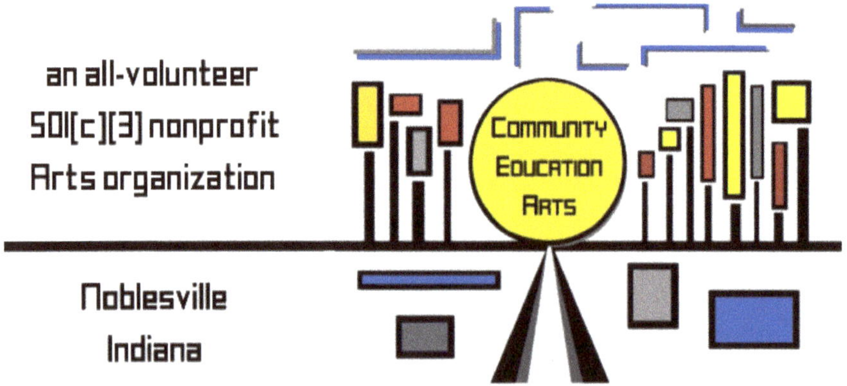

Green Santa by Sarah E. Morin

Trees,
unending trees sprouted
in his
front yard each December.
The naïve shoppers
believed the farmer sowed pinecones
on Thanksgiving and they
grew overnight instead of being painstakingly
planted, fertilized, shaped, chainsawed, hauled
in the rough-hewn wagon by his
six strapping pork-fed Hoosier sons
and tied with fraying twine to metal stakes.
He never disillusioned the city folk with
the mundane recipe of dirt, sweat, time, and luck.
Let his customers believe he was Santa in
John Deere green insulated overalls, a round-bellied wonder-worker,
perhaps his reindeer off grazing in the pasture with
the Herefords and Black Angus. Even a plain Indiana farmer yearns
for
magic.

This poem is inspired by my Grandpa, who ran a Christmas tree farm for decades and was known locally as the Green Santa. Visiting his farm was a regular Christmas tradition for many families.

Sweet and Sour by John Caviness

Not every taste is by the tongue
Some experiences are sugar at the start
And acidic in the end

To have both at once is the key
Sour-patches
Skittles
True love

Untitled 2 by Audrey Barcio

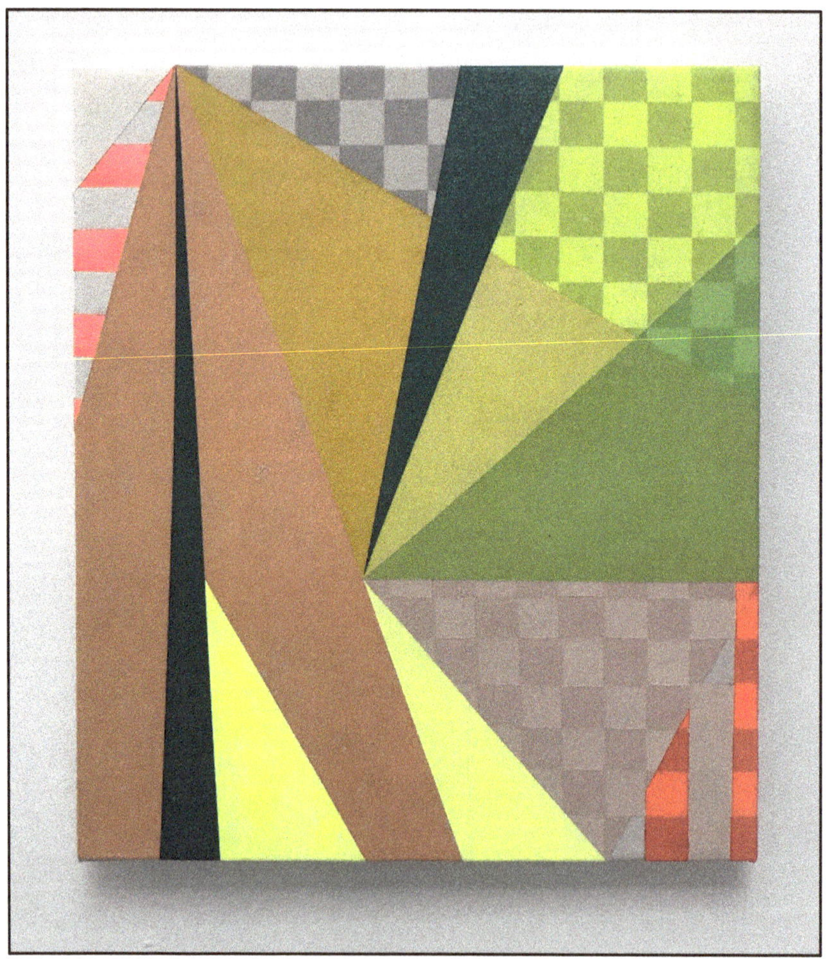

Ode to the Comet NEOWISE by George W. Wolfe

You seemed innocent enough, a whisper of light against the deep sky. Holding my binoculars steady, I was lured into a magnified moment made breathless by wonder. You floated above the northwest horizon, as if the Big Dipper's ladle had overflowed.

But humanity discovered you too late, O Kuiper messenger of doom. Our pandemic infested planet is now writhing in poverty and politics, pollution and pain. The sword of your tail slices through reason, masking responsibility as you move through warped space, deceiving us into blaming you, rather than ourselves.

The light of the moon by John Caviness

Lazily rise, o ball of light in night
Wash over the land and sea gleaming
Flit and fleet about the shadows in spite
Chart your course, through the sky unending

Calmly rejoice, o awakened beasts nocturnal
Scour your territories and caches heaping
Fight and escape your enemies infernal
Take your time, the night is retreating

Lazily fall, o blemished mother of night
Rest, wash over the land and sea far reaching
Wax and wane from the sun in spite
Chart the next course, through the sky awaiting

Bicycle by Deborah J. Peterson

I loved my grandfather.

He gave me a freedom and permission and a rite, gifts unmatched by any other. He bought me my first and very own bicycle. It was not the kind with the banana seat or with plastic tails attached to the hand grips; no, it was a Foremost, kinda greenish and white (later, I learned the proper name was "turquoise") and unlike any other. Sure, there were bicycles all around, no doubt, with 14 kids total in our house and the one across the street. We shared bikes for there did not seem to be ownership of the ones sprinkled about our yards, left in the rain, in all sorts of disrepair and mobility. But, here was mine, and mine alone.

It was a bike that did not have gears or speeds; its power and speed was determined by the number of minutes we were late after curfew or trying to outrun the storm and lightning hits. With a bike, we all became pre-pubescent engineers: "You're on your own, kid, best learn how to change that tire!" I knew how to replace a slipped bike chain and make adjustments to the seat and handlebars for just the right height. I knew how to attach the wire baskets to the back so that I could deliver newspapers, and pick up milk, Kool-Aid, bread, and bologna at the store.

In the summer, all the days were the same: Tuesdays were Thursdays, Fridays were Saturdays. We had to rely on the adults to tell us when the school year was coming back around and the day long bike adventures were coming to a close. It was unheard of to ask an adult to drive us anywhere. The mornings would start early (not aware of any time on the clock, just the shadows of the leaves coming into the kitchen as the sun was rising), gulping down some breakfast cereal after a fight with the siblings over who was going to get the toy inside the box, which always broke by the end of the day, whether it was a magic code ring, or spinning top, or ball in a maze. Then, up and out onto the street with freedom and summer street heat and breezes when we found the hill to glide down real fast. No helmets. No water bottles. No food. We knew where most garden hoses were kept and adults always had some fruit or a peanut butter sandwich ready to hand out wherever we landed.

If there was a plan to spend the day with a friend or a cousin, we were on our own and wore the confidence in getting where we needed to go like the dirt sweat ring on our necks. We didn't measure distances by miles back then, no, it was more by the number of dreams, and songs we belted out from beginning to end by the Monkees and Paul Revere and the Raiders. One day, we headed out to the Eckert's for horseback riding. Another day, to collect eggs out at the Kennedy's chicken farm. Some days, we headed north, then east to spend the day making cannon ball jumps in the quarry in the back 40 at the

Warner's. Then, there were the days to bale hay at the Christman's and to milk cows at the Hoffman's. I had heard, some time ago, there was a culture somewhere on an island in the Pacific that did not have different words for "work" and "play"– funny, neither did we in this small Midwestern town.

They say "A dirty child is a happy child" and they said right. I recall the playground conversations once school started up again and showing off the war wounds of the season, the bumps and bruises of bicycle wrecks, the scars earned from the adventures and the freedom, and the permission from the season's rites of passage. Looking back, I do believe that my bicycle took me to my first kiss, and to places where the cool kids hung out, until, we didn't.

Thanks so much, grandpa!

Ball-Ball (aka, Our Backyard's Waiting For You) by Alys Caviness-Gober

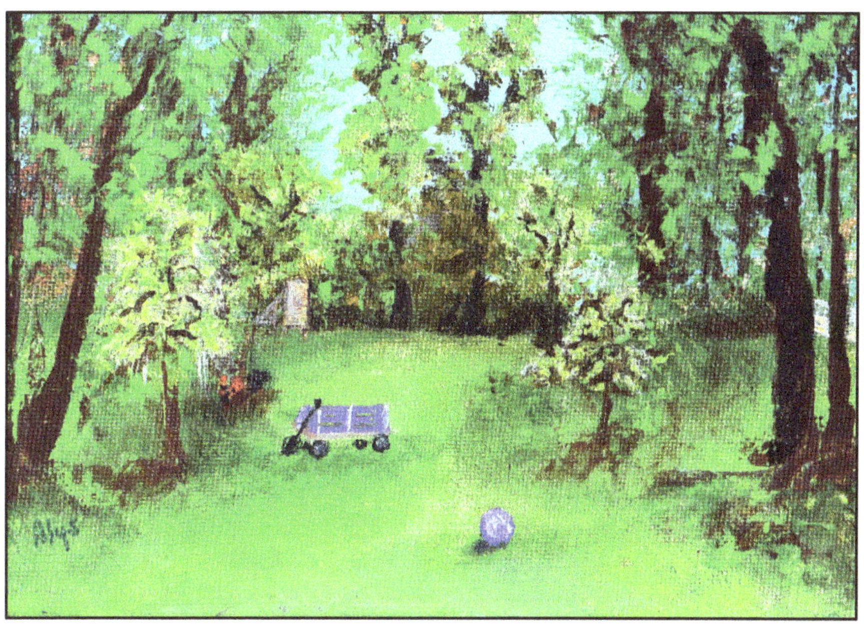

Thanksgiving Ghosts by Bonita Cox Searle

I love the stillness before
that first knock,
our home clean to the corners,
the table laid with
delicate
china bowls from
grandmothers before me,
the air thick
with Thanksgiving.

I wait for
your brother and sister
to come through the front door,
their families dancing
into our arms,
and filling our home with
laughter and
chaos.

In that stillness,
as I wait,
I conjure you here
with your family that
never was.

You have a cheeky boy with
your cheeky grin and
a small girl who runs when
she should walk.

His name is Benji,
I've decided and hers,
Hope or maybe
Gracie.

And there by your side,
I glimpse the partner
you never met and he,
like me,

loves you more than
you ever loved
yourself.

Sailboat (June 2011) by George Wylie

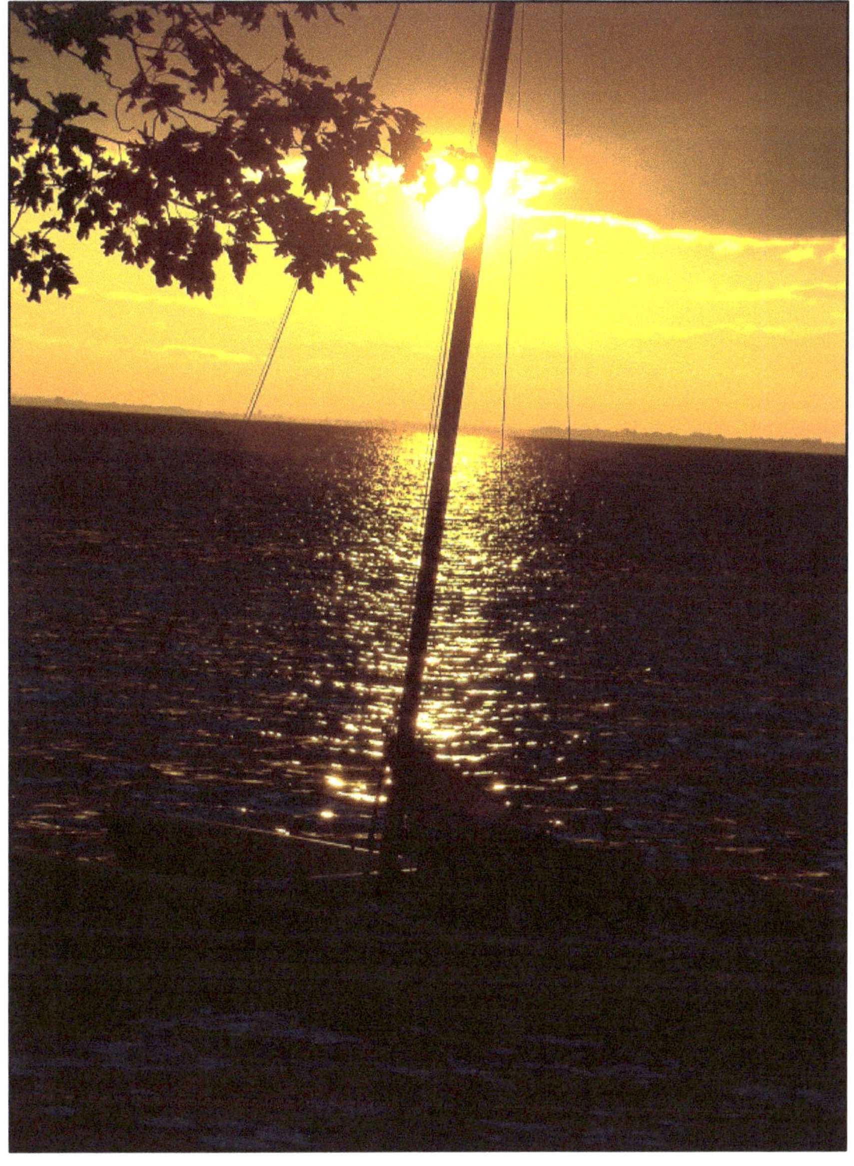

When Will They Notice by John Caviness

Mass propagation of continuous signals
lost in digital
lost to the following
missed by the mourning.

Video cameras caught the whole thing
wrought by hatred
pressed to the ground
crushed by The Man.

Everyone saw it.
The people rioted.
How many must die
for society to notice

the deaths of thousands
at the hands of protectors.

She. Is. Salve. by E. A. Wasonga

She says things that make me want to grab a pen and write again.
She talks and uses terms like the history of women in sentences or
inspires me to title pieces as *Girl Child Raised By A Rebel Man.*
She talks of being useful to more than ourselves and our immediate
family.
She is familiar with the necessity of duty when afforded life.

She talks of how things were when she was a child.
She shares what it was like to imagine being a woman then.
Education was simply to make women interesting spouses.

The way the sun rose in her days was very different.
We are a decade and some change apart in years.

The changes that came about between her birth and mine makes me
want to call certain groups of mankind to a press conference and
announce how rapidly Africa grows and becomes, but that is a war for
another day.

She makes me feel safe in my difference because we share what it's like for both of us.

She makes me feel like I have an ally in a world that is busy doing things and not asking why.

She makes my spirit as tall as our ancestors were when they lived in The North.
I always pray that those who changed state and left before us, as well as The Universe that allowed us, surround her and keep her well for many, many, many more moons.

My nakedness is safe in these gardens with her and even if she were to disappear, because most of the people that happen upon my life are seasonal or spread across too much of the earth … I would still be able to keep going from the amount of everything she has poured into me.

She empowers me not just for her company, and for this time.
She empowers my tomorrows and the tomorrows of my children as well.

When I am with her, we become more and more of what the earth needs.
She. Is. Salve.

With her, women aren't just misunderstandings, gossip, and unbalanced deeds.
With her, women have sense.
Women understand and pursue purpose.
Women can be, and are, rebels … clothed in peace and the truthfulness of God that got lost between prophets and organized religion.

I am grateful to have met her by blood and to have remained with her into the dawn's after forgiveness became our shields, spears, and wings.

I dedicate this poem to the healers of the world that understand scales will almost always be the birth of a version of war.
Here is a link to the poem on YouTube:

https://www.youtube.com/watch?v=bnBfqrHslJI
Art to go with *She. Is. Salve*. poem:
Credit to Jasvir: Instagram.com/soullpainting

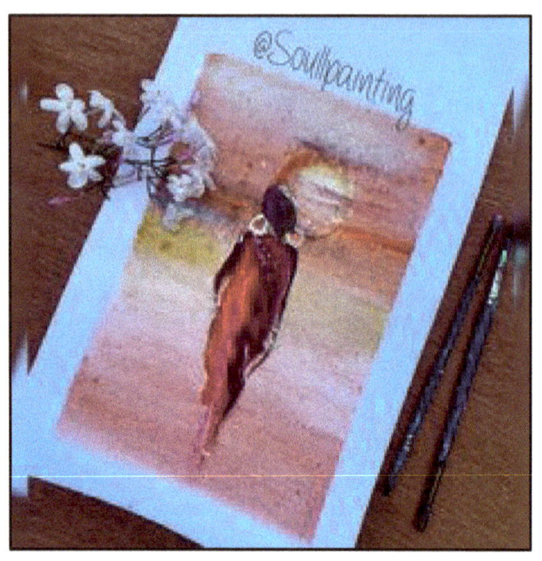

A Christmas Haiku by George W. Wolfe

Choirs sing "Silent Night."
Bridge shelters mom with newborn.
Dark nativity.

Guilt by John Caviness

Worth it.

A rush of rotten pleasure
The resemblance of remembered times
You're going to want that
Rock and roll, salty snacks

You're going to regret it
Reality TV, chocolatey sweets

Worth it.

Keeping In Touch by Chuck Kellum

I.

Facebook feeds me
Daily news,
Complete with pictures
And conflicting views;
   All from sources
   Whom I choose.

Most are friends
But some aren't really,
And most hold back
Though some share freely
   (And often).

II.

I want a bridge
Across the gulf
Of time and place
And other/self;
   Online friends
   Most days can help.

But in the end
It's face to face
And hand in hand
In times of place,
With back and forth
And give and take,
Where memories form
At equal pace,
   To know each other
   Well.

III.

I miss you, my dear friend.

Untitled 4 by Audrey Barcio

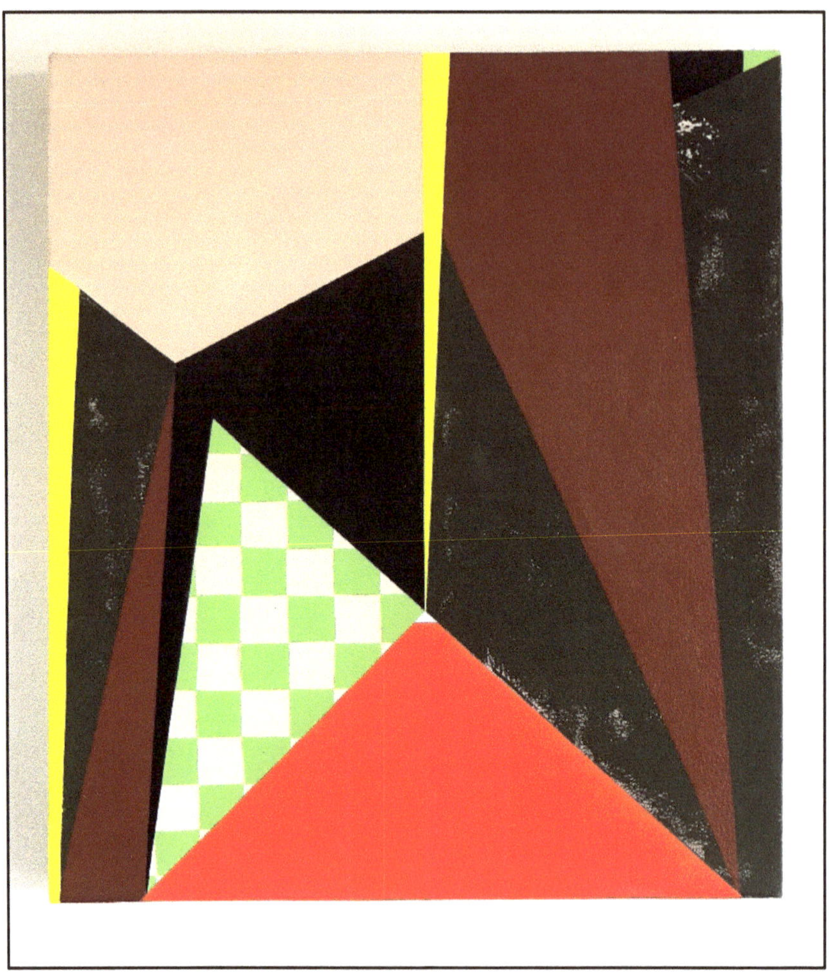

Kitchen Table by Deborah J. Petersen

Interesting fact: geographically speaking, our kitchen table was located smack-dab in the middle in our home. Not only was the house – upstairs, downstairs, front, and back – built up around this table, but our lives were grown around this table as well. It was the center of our universe in more ways than one; it was where our stories, our meals, our laughter, our tears, at times, found their way.

When my daughters were wee ones and became students, each morning the table was readied for them. On their placemat, at their particular chair, was their cereal bowl and juice glass, and spoon which cradled a chewy vitamin. Two to three choices of cereals stood in the center. After breakfast, it was hair styling time. Did we want pigtails? Curls with a ribbon? Ponytail with headband and bow? Braids with barrettes? And, what was on the day's agenda? Who will be our lunch partners? What game shall commence on the playground? What are the latest goings-on in the lives of the others at school?

Our evening meal was the time for stories, of telling the tales of the day's events, of the coming together after time apart to connect and share. It was a rite of passage, a major milestone, when each daughter turned old enough to light the Candle of Gratitude in the middle of the table, which designated the beginning of each meal. Trying to click the torch lighter just right to get the flame just right on the wick at the just right angle, was a proud moment. The light of our deep prayers of Gratitude shined extremely brightly here in the center of our lives at that moment.

On Saturday mornings, there at the kitchen table, was the Menu Planning. Starting with the calendar and lists of sports games, practices, club meetings, events, gatherings, and all the other little life celebrations, began the look and feel of the next week's menus. Away game on Tuesday – that means a crock pot meal. Friend's birthday – that means cookies were to be baked. Boyfriends for supper – best find out their favorite foods. Once the flow was established, then the cookbooks came out: new recipes, broadened palatial horizons, fun and easy, long, and detailed. What are the taste buds craving? With each menu there were items noted on the grocery list just for that week's meals; gather the coupons according to the recipes, then organize according to the aisles at the local grocery. This on Saturday morning, at the kitchen table – the planning of a lifetime, one week at a time.

Sunday afternoons were set aside for cooking the meals for the week, soup steaming the room, aromas wafting, chopping the veggies to the background music, while my daughters sat at the kitchen table and finished up the last of the homework for the next Monday.

Small celebrations took place here at the kitchen table:

- the make-your-own-ice-cream-sodas birthday parties with every imaginable scoop of topping
- the who-can-design-the-most-creative-pizza slumber parties
- the “Make-It-Or-Bake-It” Christmas holiday gifts for family, friends, and neighbors

Eventually, the kitchen table became the place for the college literature and the plans for next life chapters. We would reserve dates and times to visit many college campuses and always did that bit more research: where is the best ice cream served near this campus? So, no matter how the visit and/or Entrance Interview went, we knew there would be ice cream at the end … how sweet!

The kitchen chairs are empty now, except for this one. Cookbooks are still poured over on Saturdays and the Gratitude Candle sits in the corner, a bit dusty. This small kitchen table, at times, was bigger than the universe. I smile at the wonder of the weight it holds of the lives lived around it, of the stories, traditions, memories, meals, and minutes, and years that took place here in this center of it all.

Christmas Cheer by Warren Sidwell

Office parties with people
you hardly know.
Matching the right gift wrap
with the perfect bow.
Package after package
dropped at your front door.
Nieces and nephews in sleeping bags
in the middle of your living room floor.
Watching your daughter’s favorite movie
for the 100th time.
Putting the kids to bed
so you can have that glass of wine.

The headaches and stress
are washed away by cheer.
Merry Christmas to everyone!
Let’s do it again next year!

Run by John Caviness

Escape
Break away
Severe the sinews that bind
Forsake the past and present

Run

Dreamscape 1 by Alys Caviness-Gober

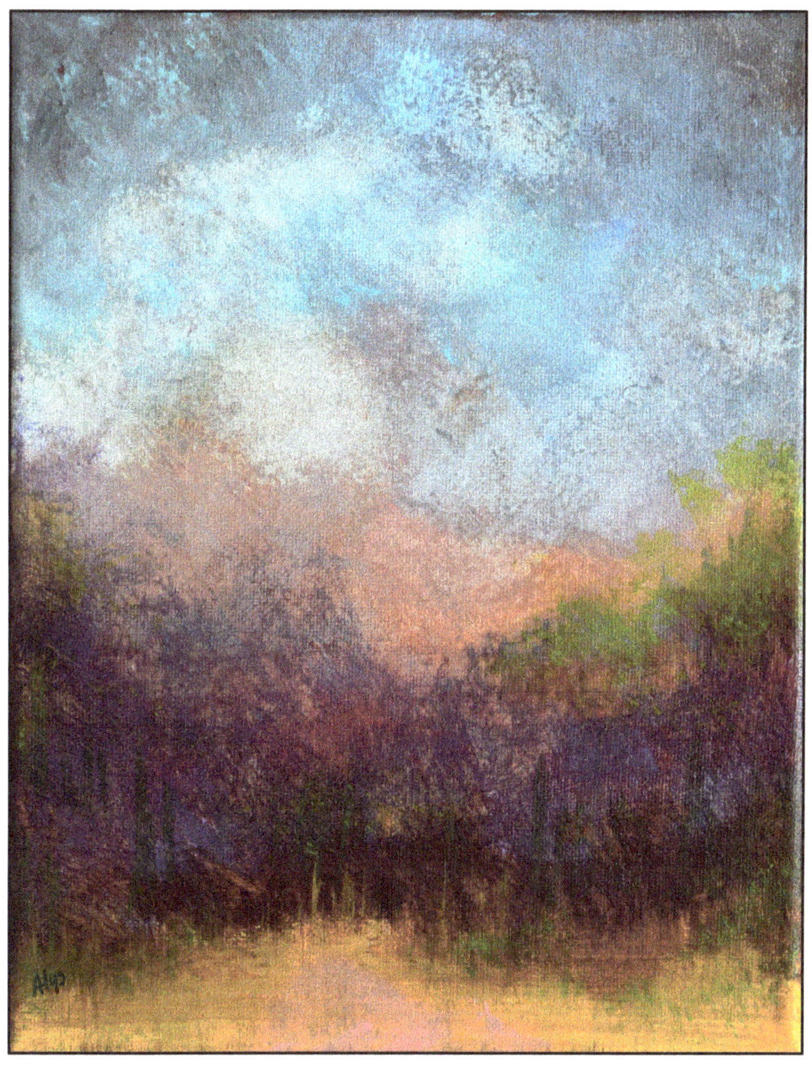

Summer Lights by Michelle "Meesh" Payne

I don't like Summertime. There. I said it. I know it's an unpopular opinion, but I have reasons to back it.

Summer is bright and shiny and even blinding at times. It's full of light. And for this night owl, I find that aspect of it a bit annoying. I'm somebody who likes mood lighting and watching TV in the dark, and I might be the only person I know who doesn't mind it when the sun sets at 5 o'clock in the wintertime. I was born on a Wednesday evening in December, so maybe that's why.

Summer Lights. There are so many types. I admire some. I highly dislike others.

The Sun – It's hot. It makes me sweat. It burns me. People say to me, "Do you ever tan?" No. I turn from white to pink back to white. I need fake tanning lotion to achieve even a hint of summer pigment. I wear my sunglasses constantly. Often indoors because I forget I have them on.

Fireworks – They're loud. They hurt my ears. I try to like them, but I don't. They're boring … I'll never forget the year my youngest daughter turned two, and we went to a fireworks show in Cicero, where she clung to me as if her life depended on it and repeatedly murmured in my ear how much she hated it. She likes them now at age 11. I still don't. They're bombs for fun, basically. How dumb.

Fireflies – They're cool. They're the nighttime version of a ladybug. Nonthreatening. They don't bite. They don't sting. They just flash. On & Off. They're consistent and silent yet emit a natural magic that can launch just about any middle-aged person straight back to childhood. Back to a mason jar with a metal lid punched with bug breathing holes and filled with blades of grass. Several simpler summers ago.

Campfire – I love the smell. I love the crackling. I love the multi-colored flames. I'm not great at building them. I cheat and buy the manufactured logs. (Yes, fake, like my tan.) I don't believe in being a fake person, but sometimes you gotta' fake it 'till you make it. But, even with those prefab logs that torch nice and easily, it's usually way too hot for a summertime campfire.

Tiki Torches – I'm a fan. They're festive. They serve a noble purpose in warding off The Evil Mosquito. However, the value of them is lost on my teenager, the oldest daughter. She fights with me about them. Says they look trashy in our yard. Thankfully, I'm at the glorious age where I'm over caring if someone thinks something looks trashy in my yard. So, I have two tiki torches.

The Grill – I love to grill out. Chicken. Salmon. Burgers. Veggies. An Occasional Steak. The black charcoal burns into orange embers, hot and bright, until they turn to a dull ashy gray. Then you know you're ready to cook! I love the smells and tastes of grilled food – one of the most redeeming things about summer, in my humble opinion.

Lightning – It's generally scary. I don't appreciate a good storm like many people I know. Streaks across the sky are fine, but I don't want to see one strike anywhere close. A few years ago, a blinding bolt hit practically on top of our house at the time. Everything electrical the neighbors owned got destroyed. We were lucky and got away unscathed. But each of us jumped three feet out of our skin.

Starlight/Moonlight – They're lovely. They're mild. They glow. They're never too bright. Never intense. I like them year-round, especially when there's some crazy lunar event I can witness from my porch, like a big-ass Harvest Moon. (I love the Fall.)

There is one light I'm missing this summer that's not here on my list. It's the kind I generate myself, on the inside of me. My light is feeling a bit off, a little dim. I need to fire it up. I'm not quite sure how.

I have ideas. I need motivation. Get more exercise. Get organized. Write a book, maybe.

I've got to get out of my daily robotic slump. Sleep until 9am. Awake until midnight. Working on my laptop at the kitchen table. Taking a nap. Making dinner. Watching Netflix. The Groundhog Day effect of quarantine and my extended remote work situation is rough and it's real. And it's making me a little grumpy.

I like to be out in the lights of the world. Stoplights. Overhead lights at the office. Trendy lights hanging above a restaurant booth. Ballpark lights at a minor league game. Stagelights at a concert or the symphony. A backlit movie theatre screen and the butter-colored warming light of the popcorn machine. Headlights both passing by me and guiding me to all these places.

Normalcy might light me up again. But what is normal now? Not the Old Normal. The New One requires us to hide our smiles behind our masks – and if you choose not to, what the hell is wrong with you?!? Our world is now one where we fear the places that used to bring us joy. (Shopping even at Target is stressful, not the mini vacation it used to be.) It's become one where we see our coworkers – some of our best friends – only *via* a cold digital screen.

Summer Lights! Shine on me. Convince me. Make me see my own shadow so I will know I'm the same person in this Strange New World. I can't control what happens around me. I can only control how I handle what happens around me. And I'm typically a Handler, so why am I not handling things better? Conflicts. Emotions. Struggles. They swirl around me. But that doesn't make me special. They swirl around all of us.

If only we could catch all of it in a mason jar. Seal it up. No breathing holes. Trap the hard stuff that we don't want to handle. And toss it in the White River under the light of the moon, or at least in the glow of a good-quality flashlight.

Or maybe we just learn to handle it. Wear the mask. Stay home, be safe, and learn to enjoy it. Grab an afternoon nap when you might otherwise be commuting an hour home from work. Hang out with your immediate family on the front porch under the flames of your tiki torches.

If your light is flickering unreliably, it's okay. So is mine. Even with all these Summer Lights shining all over the place.

Bring me cooler and dimmer days, and, ironically, that might brighten my flame. Until then, I'll be over here soaking up the A/C and shaming Summer.

***Author's Note*:** As the grand finale to my Summer 2020, I contracted

COVID-19 in mid-August, after I wrote this piece. As you can imagine, that dimmed my flame big time and made summertime even harder for me than this entry expressed. Thankfully, I stayed out of the hospital and simply struggled through my illness at home for about 3 weeks. I wrote another piece about that experience which can be found on my blog - www.iamnotyourmom.com – and it's titled *Not Your Mom's Guide to Coronavirus.*

Break the social taboo – talk about mental health by John Caviness

A man is meant to show only a few things:
strength, anger, and power, but
that makes a man weaker.

The human condition requires more:
to feel is to live,
to hurt is to grow,
suppression is the expectation
but the answer is expression.

The Sweater by Jenny Kalahar

After my grandpa passed away
Mom said she wanted one thing from his closet:
a rust-brown cardigan he'd worn for years
with moth holes sewn over in zigzag stitches
the hem stretched
buttons that didn't quite match.
She wore it as often as Grandpa
taking over a part of his skin or bones or essence.
At first, I wondered why my dad never wore it
never wanted to carry on his father's tradition
and why my mom very much did.

I have a photo of Grandpa on his sun porch
newspaper open at lap level
his horn-rimmed glasses framing his eye's secret merriment
and that cardigan keeping him warm for the first hours of the day
the ball field in the background through the windows

me at the table a few feet away in pigtails,
slurping cereal
happy to be right there with my grandparents
woolly-warm and loved.

When my mother hugged me wearing that sweater
the particular scratch of the shoulder against my cheek
transferred some of the affection I had for Grandpa
into my mom
like a magnet drawing that distinctive brand of love
from my heart to hers.
And now I understand –
the borrowance
was her way of keeping Grandpa's love flowing into me
using the still-earthly instruments of her arms.

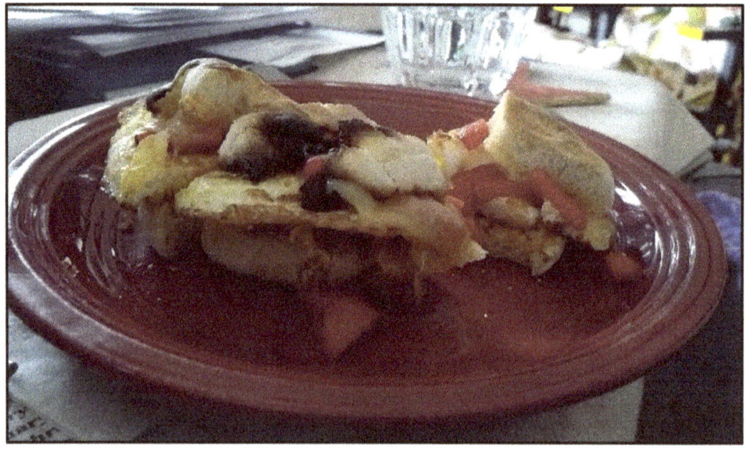

Variations on a (recipe's) theme: Moonstruck Eggs by Alys Caviness-Gober

I love the movie *Moonstruck*, and here's my simple (and delicious!) take on the famous *Moonstruck Eggs*:

> One egg fried in butter, topped with chopped roasted red peppers and a slice of Havarti cheese, sandwiched in a toasted English muffin.

Saying Goodbye by George Wylie

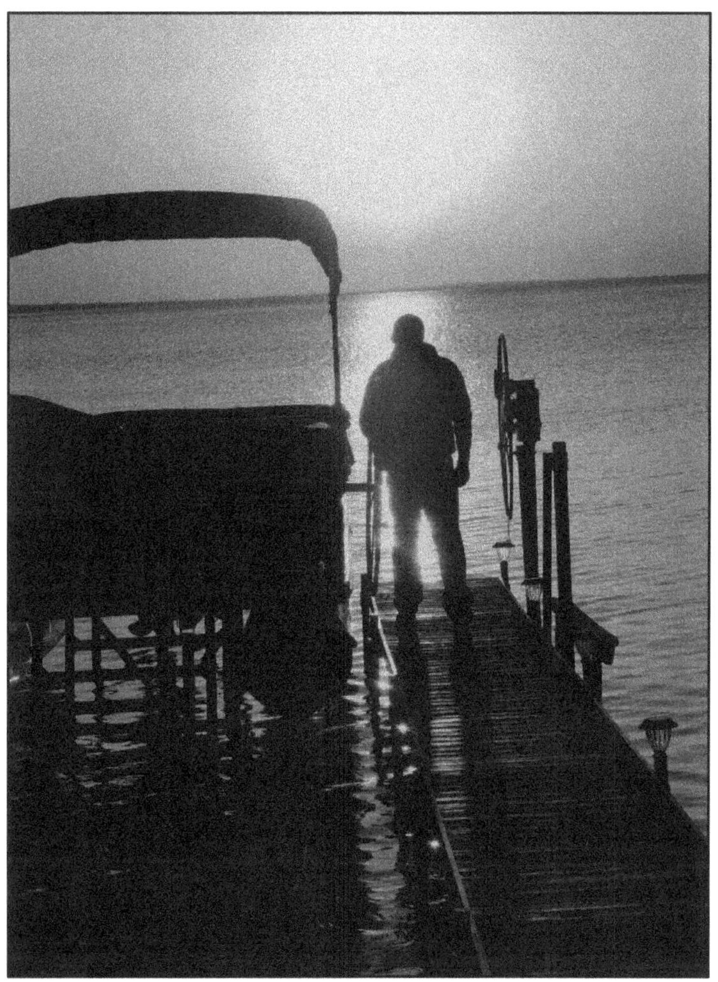

Did you feel that? by John Caviness

Biting one's tongue
seeing the signs,
the beat of two lives
strutting towards that moment,
steps in milliseconds
two faces react,
eyes meet and close.

Did you feel that?

Consoling the Moon by Michael E. Strosahl

As you walked away,
I caught the moon in reflection,
wondering what life would be
as you continued
over the horizon and into tomorrow.

I have to admit,
there were no words to offer,
there was no comfort I could give
to a moon so full of sorrow,
on a night that
never seems to end
beside the waters silently washing
our last moments
down to the river
and off to the sea.

Rita In Her Heaven by George Wylie

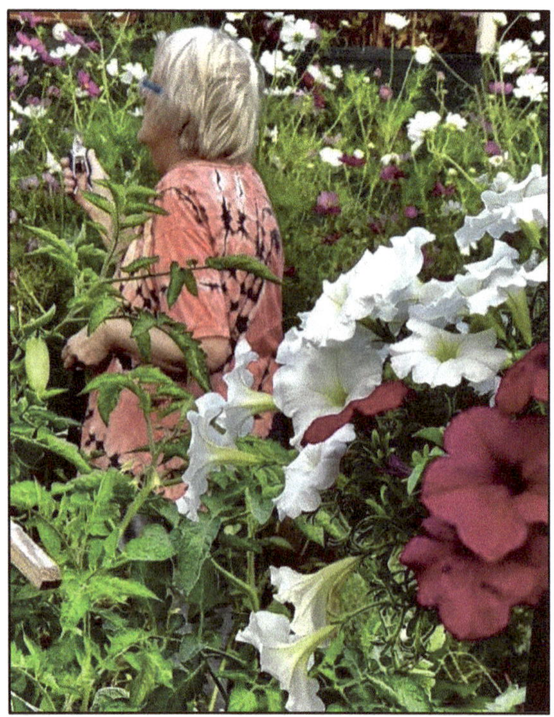

That Is How High He Was by Ndaba Sibanda

He said he was praying in tongues
When he was taking hard drugs
"I ask not to be disturbed please
As my court of fun is in session!"

Language Of Angels by Deborah J. Petersen

Adeste Fideles
Early winter was the season of
Purple and pink candles,
And old stories –
We sang in the language of angels
Our harmony, we knew, came from heaven;

Laeti triumphantes
It was Midnight Mass in the cathedral
And a time to wear our new dresses and don our new shoes
As mightily as youth could take us.
A place in the choir, up where the angels fly.

Natum videte
This was our sacred and secret language;
This was our direct connection to the Divine;
This was our moment of Grace and
Knee-shaking faith come alive.

Regem angelorum
The words, no longer sung.
The shoes, no longer fit.
But, the gifts of the wonder of Awe and
The love of Ritual, Bless me still.
Amen.

Inktober 2020 Day 1 Fish by Andrea Haydon

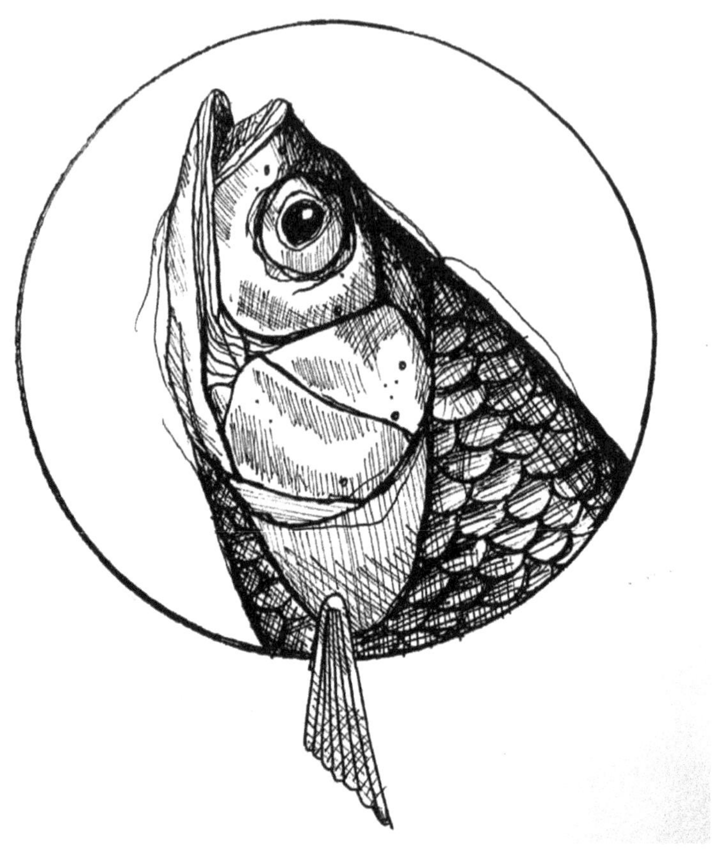

Looking Forward by Vivianne Belle

A New Year means certain rituals for me. In the week after Christmas, I'd make a list of New Year Resolutions, like

- Eat fewer sweets ("fewer" being a relative term; a resolution that's not so easy if you have a sweet tooth like I do).
- Walk more (walking being the easiest of all dreaded forms of exercise).
- Be nicer (in a vague, general way).
- Clean out my closets (to give stuff to charities).

On New Year's Eve, I'd dress up and go out with friends to crowded bars and/or town squares, where we'd all:

- drink copious amounts of alcohol
- wear silly shiny paper hats
- blow annoying noise-makers directly into each other's faces
- join in the group countdown to the New Year
- kiss someone (often a random stranger) as the last bell of midnight rang
- drunkenly sing Auld Lang Syne

These rituals, these traditions, started when I turned 21 and continued for the next couple of decades. Friends and places changed as I moved around, of course, but the basics remained. I remember there were a few years when New Year's Eve celebrations transitioned to someone's house, accommodating friends who had small children. Even then, the list above remained much the same. There were fewer strangers to randomly kiss at the stroke of midnight, but it was still a possibility.

Those were the days, ay?

Then came a global pandemic, an incredibly contagious novel coronavirus, COVID-19 (in this context, *novel* means *new*). It hit in earnest, with no discrimination for borders or persons in early 2020, and for the rest of the year took a horrible human toll across the world. Some countries fared better than others because they initiated lockdowns and mandatory mask-wearing in March and April.

In America, then-President Trump, who over the past four years revealed himself as a racist fascist wannabe dictator, intentionally misled the American people about the very real threat: he lied about it from January 2020 right up through the November election m(and ignored it completely after losing the election by an unprecednted landslide). From the get-go, he used the pandemic to divide the country by politicizing the virus. He publicly called it a "hoax," mocked mask-wearers, derided health officials and scientists and scientific facts about the virus, refused to cooperate with the World Health Organization, manipulated the Centers for Disease Control, told his supporters that mask-wearing was an infringement on their "freedom," held maskless rallies and meetings, and tweeted about bizarre junk science.

The numbers of infected and dead in America by the end of 2020 are a sad and now historic matter of record. Under Trump's administration, COVID-19 decimated the economy: the staggering numbers of the unemployed, the unimaginable increase in the number of men, women, and children made homeless, and the forever closed businesses are all also a matter of sad historic record.

Hope dawned across America after the election of President-elect Joe Biden and Vice President-elect Kamala Harris, but as I write this, we're still 20-some days away from the inauguration, and Trump hasn't yet conceded. He is still actively trying to "take over" the country; he continues to stoke the flames of racism and sedition.

Those of us who took the virus seriously from the beginning did everything we could to minimize risk to ourselves and others: we wore masks, we socially distanced, we didn't get together in person for birthdays or holidays. Those of us lucky enough to have jobs that allowed us to work at home have spent most of 2020 in front of our computers, working, Zooming meetings, and rarely going anywhere.

I'm one of those fortunate folks, rattling around in my little cottage, working, Zooming … and, like everybody else, feeling the hours and days just flow into each other like ocean waves. As this crazy year – this first year of COVID-19 – comes to an end, I write out my New Year's Resolutions.

They are similar to my old ones, and after almost a year of not going anywhere, I resolve to

- Eat less. (good lord, isolation includes almost constant eating)
- Walk more (masked, even after getting a vaccine).
- Be nicer. (we all need to be nicer to each other, don't you?)
- Clean out my closets. (wearing "good" clothing is a thing of the past; I'm happy with casual tops and elastic waistbands)

As for my New Year's Eve celebration, gone – possibly forever? – are my old partying-with-friends rituals. Instead, I'm going to

- put on my oldest and comfiest flannel pajamas
- make myself a pitcher copiously full of a festive cocktail of some sort (researching festive cocktails has been a rather fun down-the-rabbit-hole internet time-waster this year!)

- watch some favorite old movies and TV shows on my streaming channels

I probably won't even notice when the last stroke of midnight rings out, I certainly won't be kissing anyone, and I seriously doubt I'll remember to sing *Auld Lang Syne*, no matter how drunk I am.

Haiku – Bourbon by John Caviness

O BOURBON! And lips
bring back those times long gone.
A drink. A drink. Up!

Dracula's Chicken Goo by Alys Caviness-Gober

In Bram Stoker's famous book, *Dracula* (1897), Jonathan Harker partakes of a chicken paprikash dish as he is travelling to Dracula's castle: "*I had for dinner, or rather supper, a chicken done up some way with red pepper, which was very good but thirsty. (Mem., get recipe for Mina.) I asked the waiter, and he said it was called 'paprika hendle,' and that as it was a national dish, I should be able to get it anywhere along the Carpathians.*"

Chicken paprikash, a traditional Hungarian stew, is thick and velvety with the subtle flavors of paprika and sour cream. Here's my version:

Dracula's Chicken Goo

PREP TIME: 15 minutes
COOK TIME: 50 minutes
TOTAL TIME: 1 hour 5 minutes

Ingredients:

- 2 tablespoons grapeseed oil
- 6-8 cloves garlic, finely chopped
- 1-2 pound chicken boneless, skinless chicken thighs
- Salt
- Freshly ground black pepper

- 2 tablespoons salted butter
- 2 yellow or white onions, thinly sliced into strips or chopped
- Optional: 1-2 red and/or orange bell pepper, thinly sliced into strips or chopped (my image is without peppers; some people can't digest them easily)
- 1-2 packs/boxes button mushrooms, sliced or chopped
- 4 tablespoons Hungarian or sweet paprika
- 2 cups chicken stock
- 1 cup sour cream
- 2 tablespoons all-purpose flour
- 6 ounces egg noodles, cooked (you could sub in rice, potatoes, späetzle, dumplings, or bread)

Instructions:

- Heat the oil in a Dutch oven or stockpot over medium-high heat.
- Pat the chicken dry, then lightly salt and pepper it on both sides. Brown the chicken, about 4 minutes per side. Set aside.
- Lower the heat to medium, then melt the butter in the Dutch oven.
- Stir in the onion, garlic, bell peppers, along with a sprinkle each of salt and pepper.
- Cook for a minute ot two, then stir in the paprika.
- Cook for about 5-7 minutes more until softened, stirring occasionally, then lower the heat to medium.
- Add mushrooms and cook, stirring often, until browned.
- Return the chicken to the pan and pour in the stock.
- Cover and bring to a simmer, then continue to cook for 25-30 minutes until the chicken is very tender and can easily be pulled apart with a fork.
- Turn the heat down to low.
- Whisk the sour cream and flour together in a small bowl.
- Stir about ½ cup of the pan sauce into the sour cream mixture so the sour cream won't curdle. Gently stir the sour cream mixture into the pan and cook for 2-3 minutes more.

Serve the chicken paprikash on egg noodles, rice, späetzle, dumplings, etc., or just dunk in thick slices of buttered bread. Enjoy!

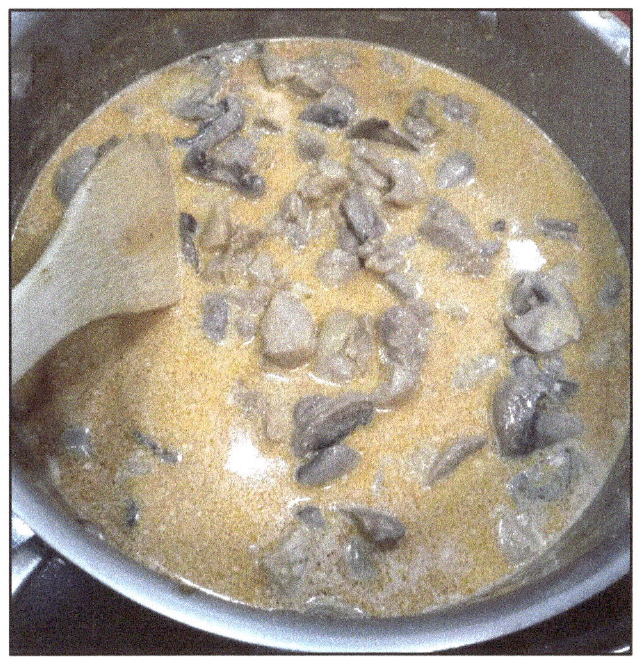

The Touch Of Greeting And Goodbye by Chuck Kellum

I.

From the caress given the newborn
  placed nearest its mother's heart,
To the warm hand laid briefly
  on one that's coffin-cold,
And in the countless many instances
Of interaction in between,
We often feel a need to touch
When we meet
Or must
Depart.

And when that can't be done
For reasons we don't control
Or isn't
For ones we do,

It may feel wrong
  (perhaps we even feel wronged)
In a deficit
Difficult to accept.

But when, upon arrival
Or in preparation for taking leave,
With welcome exchange
We embrace someone we love
  or very much like,
Or clasp the hand of a perfect stranger,
Or rub noses, as in the Inuit lands,
Or, according to European fashion, brush cheeks
  with puckered lips,
Or perform such rites of direct contact
  in whatever other manner appropriate,
It simply
Feels right
And good
And the way
Things always have been
And should be.

II.

Your cheek to my cheek
And your arms enfolding me
Say more than words
You're here right now
And would stay
Without want to go.

A Cappella by George W. Wolfe

The doors were heavy, hard
for a six-year-old to open. I
stared at the gray floors as my
mother led me to class. Inside, I
was dodging shadows, hiding
from hallways, trying to
bury my fears of separation.

Miss Young welcomed me to the
first grade. I couldn't see her smile
through blurry eyes. That year
she'd teach me to read and to add,
to play dodge ball and to write
my name, but it was my mother
who taught me to sing.

In spring the two would stroll among
the iris, Mother's words coloring the
light with evening moods. Miss Young
could name every blossom, like the
children in her class. My dog and I
rambled through the garden. I'd throw
a ball into the neighbor's yard for him
to fetch. We weren't interested in
flowers.

As the years passed the shadows
grew longer while her memory
wilted. Mom finally sold the house.
Yet her song still lingers, even
without a beating heart.

Shackles by John Caviness

Tied up, waiting for what's next.
Built up, watching the other set the fate.

Anticipation in the mystery.
Immolation of the wick.
The only source of light.

Unlocked.
Unbound.
Released.

Sniffing To Awareness by Deborah J. Petersen

Our Worship Service –
Strolling the Rivergreenway.
You, my four-legged friend,
Pulling me along the asphalt path
As we are caught up in
The soft wind, serenaded by the
Giggling leaves.
This is our Sweet No-Time.
This is us flexing and dancing our muscles.
Turtles are basking on the shore in the sun's heat;
And, the cranes are swooping for food.
This could be any day, any year –
Unchanging, constant.
I follow you and pay close attention.
You stop, muzzle through the patch of grass
Detecting the geese's recent visit.
You teach me to stop and
Be aware,
Fully aware.
Thank you, dear friend.
Thank you for showing me how to
Awaken to the Divine.

Kit and Micki: Peace is Possible by Noah R.

Hi, my name is Noah. I am 12 years old and I attend Noblesville East Middle School. I would like to introduce the world to my pets Kit, and Micki.

A lot of people believe cats and dogs cannot get along. I have come to find that this isn't always true. Don't get me wrong, Kit and Micki do have their moments. Kit is naughty and forever interested in playing. Micki likes her nap, and eating from everybody's plate. This means that from time to time they often fight. Especially when Kit wants to play but Micki would prefer a nap, or when Micki wants to see what Kit is having for lunch but Kit would prefer not to share because Kit has his own bowl.

The other day, though, while Kit was basking in the sun and chasing squirrels, a bigger, older cat came to bully Kit. Luckily, Micki heard the commotion and rushed outside to investigate the matter. Micki quickly analyzed the situation; she rose to her brother, Kit's, defense. Together, they chased away the bigger, older cat that was bullying Kit in his own yard. After their victory, they strolled back into the house together.

This taught me that cats and dogs are able to get along and perhaps the narratives we are used to don't have to be the only law of the land.

I think we can learn a lot from Kit and Micki.

Is there someone, or a group of people, you do not agree with on world views? Perhaps the focus should not be on your differences, but rather on what you can work on together to make the world be a better and safer place for all.

The Loneliness of His Discontent by George Wylie

He had taken to looking out windows more
but the world out there seemed to have no interest in him.
Fewer cars spattered by on his wet leaf-strewn street.
One morning an ambulance had come to the gray house on the corner
and he wondered if old Edna would ever return.
The barbershop had taken on a quiet pall with only one person at a time
and he wondered about the value of his sterilized haircut that no one sees.
At the store the many masks seemed to also become muzzles
and fewer words were spoken, as if they were told that talking was lethal.
And someone else arrived every day to walk Edna's dog.
That he would not be invited to a holiday dinner with family
was expected and it made great sense that he declined.
Who knew what dangers lay in Aunt Marie's hug
or Brenda's sweet rolls or the nicely lined up silverware?
Would it have been smart to pet their dog?
He washed his hands, again. On the windowsill was a prayer card

from Uncle Walt's funeral, meager as it was, in a windy tent with only nine people.
Walt's own priest had died and they used a rent-a-pastor for the lonely rite.
The man apologized for not knowing Walt, or anyone else there.
He tried to care.
And the disinterested leaves skittered across the cold slope of arranged stones and fake flowers.
He decided to buy a small turkey and the other stuff it requires.
He cooked it carefully as she had always told him to. It had to be safe of course.
With a rampant monster virus all around, one could hardly dare to get ill from food.
Alone at the table, he tried a spoonful of cranberries and stared at the dead bird,
brownly golden on a fine platter of sweet smells.
For some reason he couldn't raise a knife to this glistening sweet skin.
He couldn't penetrate the shape and spirit of this familial comrade.
He took a bite of green beans and then he decided not to violate the turkey.
He covered it and then went to the window where it was getting colder and darker.
There was a *For Sale* sign in Old Edna's lawn.

Conquer by John Caviness

tear into the enemy
relent for nothing
the lands of plenty
wait on no one

each rise and fall
stay impending
powers to rule
stay fleeting

seizure of the moment
recognizing a place of opportunity
acknowledge the enemy
strike at the chosen

Pleasant Run In The Fall by Andrea Haydon

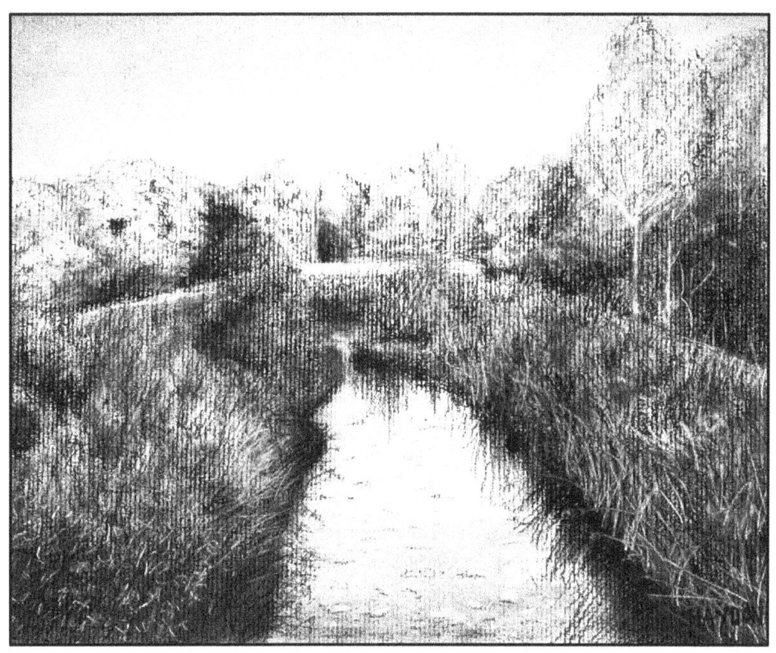

Caretaker's Melody by Jenny Kalahar

There is a soundtrack to being taken care of:
The click of spoon on bowl edge,
water running over a washcloth in the bathroom down the hall,
a toilet being flushed by another's hand,
vegetables in a blender, whirring to mush,
a game show on the television,
conversation with visitors that do not include the patient.

The day is long,
wanting to be alone yet unable to be alone for long,
slipping into memories of those who are not present,
yearning for a vacation from bed, chair, bed, chair,
wanting to anger the caretaker into leaving
but fearing their abandonment.

There is a soundtrack to being taken care of:
it sounds like a now-familiar voice
you cling to

for ties to the outside world;
It sounds like laughter.
It sounds as soothing as meaningless chatter
even though you've heard the stories
a hundred times before.

Haiku for fall by John Caviness

fall too fast, won't last
fall real slow and find the piece
give it time to grow

Man On The Pier by George Wylie

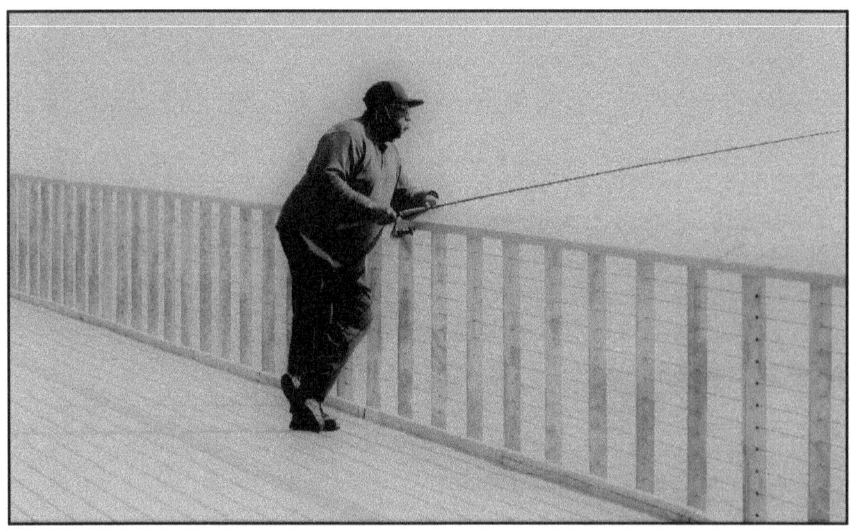

The Rains of My Nights by George Wylie

The rains of my life have been kind, and I treasure their acquaintances.
Rains to me have hue, they have a scent and a voice. They clasp on me in different ways.
Brings back youthful nights when camping and the rain pattering chopsticks on my canopy.

And serving up a rim of canvas security, tucked in my bag with big brothers nearby.
I couldn't have felt more safe and familial.
Across the decades of my life the rains have always helped me sleep.
And think.
In a bigger tents with family and smaller tents with lovers.
We looked for spots the rains come in and plug them with a laugh
If we were tired the rain was our guardian, an excuse to move in and listen.
We sipped warm beer and dozed off to the dimming chuckle of some old joke.
Escaping the flaps only to pee, we returned to shake wet shirts at our companions.
Raising the boys, I taught them the joy of rain and they learned to run into the splashes
To plunge into the warm torrent, worry not about dry clothing, try to look up into rain without blinking.
And we learned to love the thunder and rumble. We added a skylight in the family room just to see the dancing of drops on the glass. Both boys have passed their love of rain and thunder onto their progeny.
We grew a family that rains well.
Now in my later more quiet years I haven't lost my love for rain, the skittery dance of marching water.
The metal awnings add a vocal drumbeat to a rainy night and grow the volume of a timid rain.
The tintinnabulation of the drops. (Sorry.) As always I open windows to better smell the rain.
A wetted morning windowsill peeves my wife but enchants me, letting me remember.
A summer rain brings a hesitant *hors d'ouvere*, then a main course, and then it tiptoes back into the trees.

The flowers get high on the rain and later, under the following sun, they smile back up with gratuity.
Most poets metaphorically link sun with happiness and rain with turbulence and endings.
I prefer to love them both, and I try to reward each of them in kind. I go out to meet a sun and also to greet a rain.
A rain is Nature tapping at your window. You should tap back.

Fits of Ginger by John Caviness

sly moving across the table
in hand, strength of nature cooked
sharply leading a front on your senses

inhale, warmth fills your lungs
breaking down the delight
fits of ginger, and a slip of the tongue

Traditions passed down from a galaxy far, far away… by Leah Leach

When I was three months old, my father wanted to go see this new sci-fi movie that was playing in the theaters. Unable to find a babysitter, my parents took me to a crowded theater and just blindly hoped for the best.

My mother tells the tale that she was worried I would cry and she'd miss the movie because she'd have to take me out of the theater. Every time she recalls this story she says, in complete shock, "You sat on my lap the whole time and didn't make a peep." In the summer of 1977 *Star Wars* was the first film I ever saw in a theater

I don't know if it was the lights, the music, or the sounds, but since that day a dark movie theater has been my oasis, my quiet place. An innermost cave where I can be in the center of myself and at the same time connected with all the world. Seeing movies in a theater has been a tradition that I have shared with my parents, my husband, and now with my kids.

For me, seeing a movie is not just throwaway entertainment. The experience of the cinema builds empathy. Movies have been monumental in my growth as a human being. I learn something from every movie I watch, whether that is how to live a human life or what to avoid. But when it comes to the *Star Wars* films, there has always been something deeper, something much more personal. Each new adventure I ask myself, *what big lesson am I to take away this time?* I continue to be shocked by the answer.

The tradition of seeing the newest *Star Wars* movie opening weekend started with my parents (I mean, having the keys to the car helped). The first three movies from 1977 – 1983 were a constant in my childhood. My brother and I saw *Return of the Jedi* so many times that to this day when we watch it, it's as if there is an echo in our heads as we hear the line in our brains a split second before it's said on screen.

In those movies I learned about the importance of friendship, standing up for what was right, not judging people for their size, and trusting your own feelings. I also learned about death and not to fear it. Because I saw Obi Wan vanish into the air, I didn't have a hard time when my beloved uncle died in a car crash. My mother did have a hard time with it and she was hospitalized for a breakdown.

When my favorite squad of fictional rebels was on Hoth I joked that it was a documentary about how to keep your friends alive in the frozen tundra of Western Michigan. I swear I still hear the *tauntaun* noises when I see the white rolling hills where I grew up.

I ached for my own merry band of rebels. It wouldn't be until my adult years that I would really find them, and lose them, and find new ones that were just as weird as me.

I spent a lot of time in isolation with *Star Wars* as my guide in my youth. In my waking hours, I was neglected and abandoned, abused, and isolated.

I wanted Obi Wan to visit me and give me an adventure, but he only came in movies. I kept the transmission lines open, hoping one day I would be worthy enough.

But my lightsaber didn't come. The generational knowledge I was given was being processed as "what not to do," so I made up my own quest. I moved to California to learn how to make the movies that would one day change the lives of others.

Where Hoth was my childhood, Mos Eisley Spaceport was Los Angeles – "You'll never find a more wretched hive of scum and villainy."

In that hive, I did find my Han Solo. Scruffy, sarcastic, and he doesn't want you to catch him doing the right thing. But when the chips are down, he's who you count on, though he doesn't want you to. He also happened to have the same birthday week as two-thirds of the *Star Wars* opening weekend release. Which is a weird coincidence.

And I did find a patch of resistance forces that shared my same ideals and were, like me, developing their own traditions and healing from their own trauma in their own way.
We saw movies together, we passionately discussed fan theories together, and when the re-release of the *Star Wars* movies came out we were even in a *Star Wars* commercial together.

(Seriously, my future husband is featured in a *Star Wars* commercial that ran during the Superbowl to promote the 1997 re-release of the *Star Wars*. I'm standing behind him like a rebel in a leather jacket and black beret.)

When the saga returned in 1999 with *Star Wars: The Phantom Menace* I saw the film opening weekend with my then husband and our friends. I adapted the tradition across the miles by having long phone conversations with my dad and my brother.

Then 2001 flipped my life a bit. After the attacks on 9/11, my husband pulled a full Luke Skywalker and signed up for the military to do his duty and help.

With the release of the next two *Star Wars* movies, I needed them more than ever before to give me guidance. *Attack of the Clones* came out when I was pregnant with my first child. *Revenge of the Sith* was released around the time my husband was about to be sent for a second tour of Iraq.

It was clear that earlier films were about the kids and these would be about the parents. I saw the movies about the kids when I was a kid and then I was seeing the movies about the parents as a new parent myself.

I would learn how corruption, absolute power, neglect, and anger could turn you to the dark side. The biggest lesson I learned was that evil was a matter of point of view. Even an inherently greedy person who works from a selfish point of view believes he or she is doing the right thing. Sometimes that evil pushes the goodness of the world to shine brighter and balance out the world.

Fast forward to 2015. I have two pre-teen daughters and *The Force Awakens* is set to release and new heroes are emerging. Heroes hopefully my daughters can relate to. We watch all the previous movies together in preparation. I don't get in deep with explaining the mythology or the messages. I answer every question they have to the best of my ability. I brace myself if they just want a "popcorn movie" that you enjoy on the surface level. I just want to share the experience with them.

It's opening night of *Force Awakens* and my daughters are new to the idea of getting to a movie theater hours before showtime. They are a bit confused by this. They slowly see the theater fill up. They start to feel the nervous tension and anticipation. Then the lights go down. People start shushing each other during the trailers to set the tone that opening night is not for talking.

The 50-screen screen illuminates a blue sentence in a font that hasn't changed in 38 years: "A long time ago in a galaxy far, far away…"

The entire theater erupts in joyous screams and applause. My daughters turn to me. They get it now. They feel the massive surge of energy. It's as if they want me to pass the baton and induct them into the tribe.

I nod. They scream too.

For the next few hours, we are connected with something beyond fandom, something beyond ourselves. We become a shared universal experience.

What started with me as an infant has transitioned to a full tradition of re-watching every *Star Wars* movie before the new release with my children. They are now at an age where we dig deep, we talk about the life lessons, the Easter eggs, the trivia, but mostly about the emotion it stirs in each of us.

"The Force will be with you, always."
– *General Leia Organa*

Oakley by John Caviness

Lone at the wheel, roots to the pedal
breathless, the oaken, mellow at 70 miles per
the path never taken grows fonder
long rides suit intricacies of broken memories

just not over a bridge.

Roses by Andrea Haydon

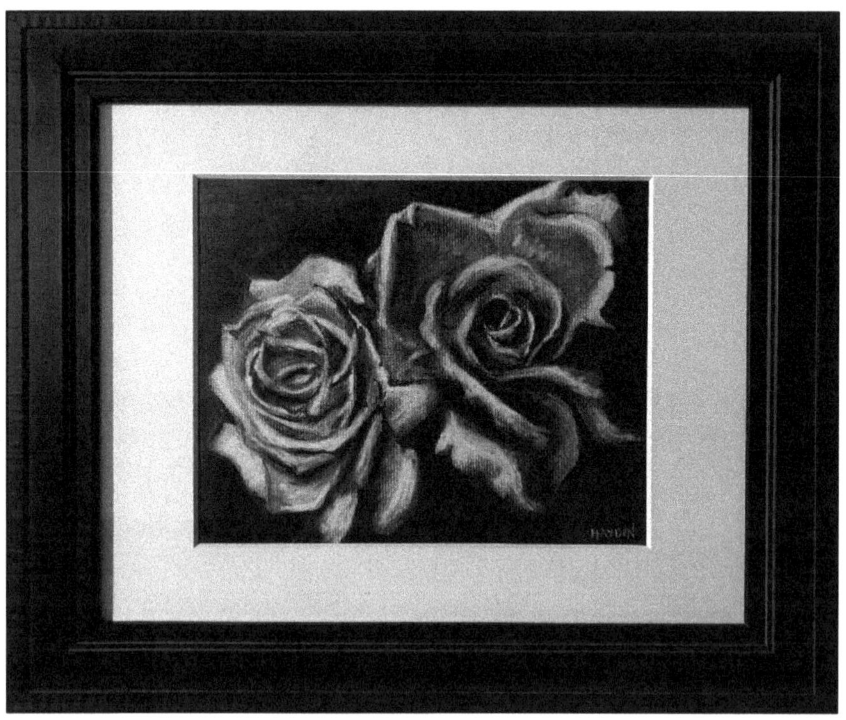

The Trials And Triumphs Of The Word Nerds by Ndaba Sibanda

A bumpy path for their pens and papers,
Alas they gathered gloom, acres and acres.

Busani and Bongile's friendship thrived,
Born of a shared love of poetry, it lived.

Busani ruled, inhabited the haiku universe.
Bongile situated her blend of free verse

Into the lived experiences of her readers.
Both grew and gloried into nerds` leaders.

6th Sense by John Caviness

A pulse increase
A cold sweat
An unexpected release

A sting of unease
A tangled net
Those trembling knees

A presence of present
A succumbing into your way
Unknown, yet an accent

Untitled by Alys Caviness-Gober

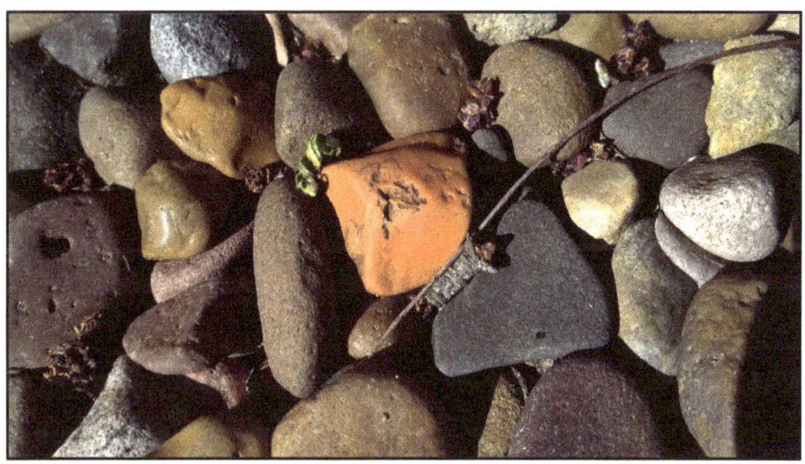

Snubbed And Stabbed by Ndaba Sibanda

Layelaye grovelled at her feet
Pleading with her to be his sweet
Yet Ngiyeke kicked him where it hurts
By virtue of his history of broken hearts

The Holiday Family Spread by George Wylie

We squeeze in extra chairs round the laden table
Cloth napkins, annual table manners
Kids cynically scanning the food
Wondering who will utter grace
And which way the food should pass
So good to see Aunt Grace
Jamie wants hotdogs
But all is good
Giving thanks
Rejoined
Full
Laughing
Did Earl shave?
Are Myrna's teeth in?
Jack's shirt has buttons!
Don't bring up politics
Is that vodka in Gail's cup?
Checking out Tad's newest girlfriend
Men are sneaking peeks at football game
What Joy! Willow says she's pregnant again!
By whom? Life's just fine at our holiday spread

Bridge haiku by John Caviness

a sight to behold
spanning the greenest wonders
path to discover

Angel Kisses by Alys Caviness-Gober

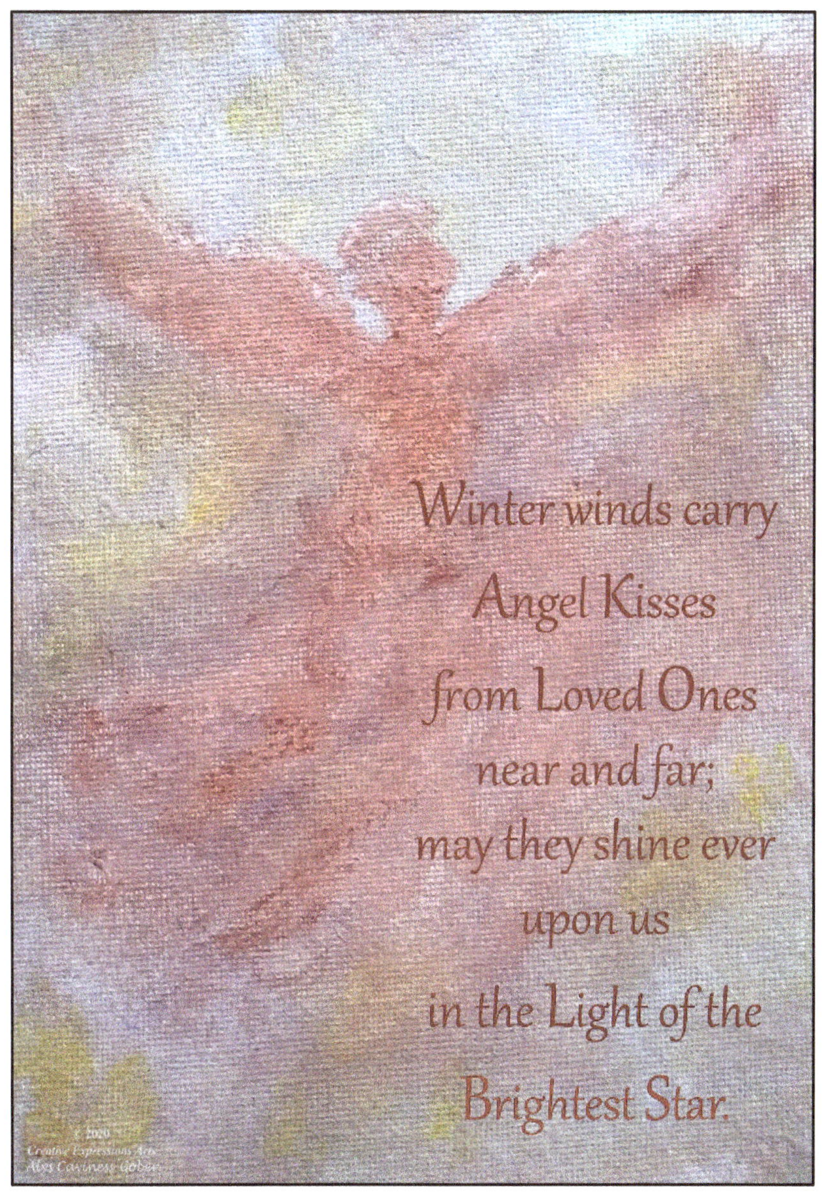

All Of It by Chuck Kellum

In all our time
Together,
Only so much

Can be said;
The rest,
Well,
We must simply
Feel
From each other.

Breathe by John Caviness

all the time
in due course
required and automatic

instantly noticed when it's gone
never missed when it's deprived

overly taken in and you'll faint
utmost importance to sustain
the blood coursing in your veins

Transitioning by George W. Wolfe
(In recognition of the hospital program, "No One Dies Alone")

It was Mother Teresa's idea, that no one
orphaned by old age should die in darkness. So
I am a bedside lamp to a much-loved
mother of two, a volunteer hand-warmer offering
a blanket of prayers until her heart chooses to
no longer sing.

I sense her soft exit. The oarsman is silent,
the river calm, except for the wake that trails
behind them. Starlight bends as the mist
enshrouds her form. I rest in this sacred
moment. Her breath passes quietly as she
departs, waiting for the moon to disappear.

Filtered Traditions by Warren Sidwell

Laughing through video screens
at parties and reunions.
Crying through masks
at weddings and funerals.

Distance does not make
the heart grow fonder.
It makes the heart ache
and miss
the warmth of
smiles and
handshakes and
hugs and
kisses.

The warmth of a touch.
Contact without filters.

Bee by Andrea Haydon

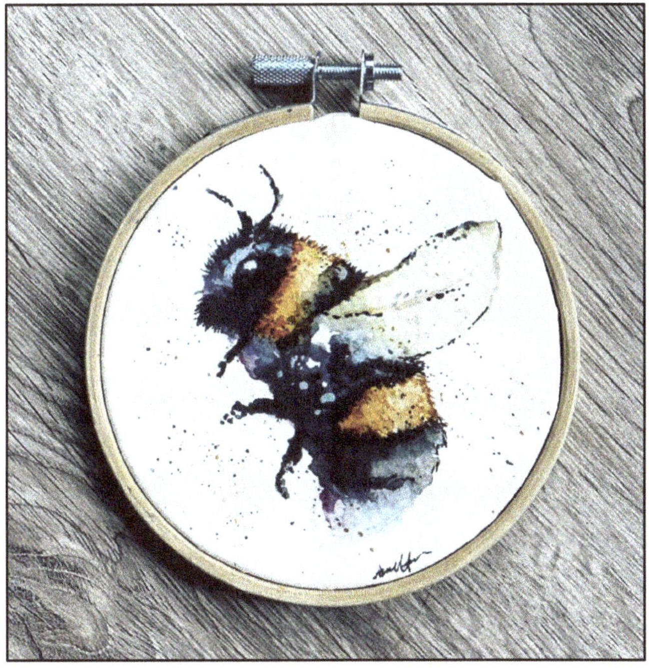

Vampires by John Caviness

Slick and pale, he entered the bar
Across the room sat a lone woman
Yellows cascade dimly on a devil's cigar
He made his approach and grabbed a stool wooden

"Two glasses of your best Bordeaux"
Eyes catch one another as the barkeep recedes
A slight attack on her mind left her a photo
Make believe and sowing seeds

Inklings of an evening elsewhere
Life without pain or strife
She felt content there
Aside him in this fictitious life

Smoke billowing between them and the glasses
Deep reds suspended by translucent grasp
A grin for her was his bypass
Now she had fallen for his trap

"Want to get out of here?"

Family Traditions – Old & New – Christmas 2020 by Kim Carlson

"Kim, your parents are crazy."

When he said this to me, I experienced an immediate disassociation from feeling this statement. Instead, I had a complete and utter understanding and validation of what I had known since I was an infant. I have no childhood memories for the most part. I mean, I have seen pictures of myself as a child and in family settings around dinner tables and the Christmas tree, but they seem so foreign to me, like they could be any pale-skinned, blonde-haired, blue-eyed child.

Except for the sexual abuse. I remember that part of it pretty clearly now.

Those memories were suppressed, however, for most of my life. They only started coming back after I began the long and painful journey back to myself through healing.

The memories of performing sexual acts on a cousin, wrestling with my father on my parents bed with him wearing nothing but his jockey briefs, walking in on my parents having sex and feeling like it was a total set up, the feeling of "him" pressed up against my back or buttocks, being in a car dressed up in my "Sunday best" reading pornographic magazines with strangers, babysitters who invited boyfriends over and give them blowjobs while I sat in the same room practicing piano, my parents throwing elaborate and extravagant dinner parties for "friends" as I was relegated to eating dinner sitting alone upstairs in front of a TV – all of that was normal adult behavior to me.

I think the fact that I have no memories of an actual good and normal childhood is representative of my childhood experience – because I didn't have good and normal experiences. And if I did, they were things I made up on my own, in a a fantasy world I created for myself.

The reality was that there was just abuse, manipulation, control, gaslighting, humiliation, lying, and ultimately my own disassociation into a world of my own making to keep me safe. I used to spend most of my time alone as a child and teenager playing, doodling, daydreaming, or listening to music.

I also remember this sort of soul-level experience from when I was born of not being loved by my parents. That was constantly confirmed to me by the stories my parents would tell to me and to anyone else who would listen, about what an awful and difficult child I was.

The profound neglect I had experienced would be revealed through the stories they told.

The stories my parents tell of me as a child all make fun of me or paint me out to look crazy or dysfunctional … but I could always see through them to the neglect and abuse that they actually revealed. My mother literally told me she used to throw me into my crib because I cried too much. I think that's what he meant when he told me my parents were crazy. It was the kindest and most gentle way to tell me that I had never been loved or really cared for – even abused and tortured – by my own parents. And when that is your first experience of love and family there can only be distortion and confusion from that point on in life.

When that is your template for what intimacy, bonding, family, and love are you literally have no choice but to choose dysfunction over and over again. It's why you don't see the "red flags" everyone talks about in other people, or know what boundaries actually are. You have been groomed and conditioned to be totally unaware. So, my experience of love and family was what you would call the cycle of abuse, until I was allowed to see it a different way and make the choice to leave it behind.

That's what I've been doing for the past two years: healing from abuse, learning what healthy love is, and defining myself as an individual worthy of boundaries and goodness in my life. Forgiveness is a tricky dance when it comes to my family/parents/abusers. I can get past and work through my triggers, sadness, and anger about all of it, but I'm acutely aware that means I have to let them go completely.

For years I held onto the belief that they could change or become the versions of them that I created as a child in my fantasy world to keep me safe. And maybe they will, someday, but that doesn't make me want to have anything to do with them. So, does that make me a bad person or someone who has been unable to truly forgive? Maybe. I don't really know.

What I do know is that since I have let them go, I have found and met other people that truly feel like the family I had been making up in my mind's daydreams. It has been an exquisite experience, to finally find and feel what unconditional love really is, and to not have to be the only one giving it in relationships. It's like the beautiful and mutual sense of knowing, appreciation, loving, and cherishing that I have been seeking out in my fantasy world has come true.

So, is forgiveness simply the act of completely letting go? Or is letting go the ultimate act of forgiveness? Or are they one in the same? Again, I don't really know at this point in my life. To be honest I don't really care, because I have finally found a family among what most people would consider complete strangers … but these strangers FEEL LIKE HOME. And that's all that matters to me. This Christmas morning was the first one where I actually woke up to the most amazing gifts I could have ever wanted – text messages from all my new friends telling me how much they loved and appreciated me, and how grateful they were to know me and have me in their lives. The feeling is completely mutual.

Perhaps the greatest gift to me is being able to return that love and appreciation back to them in real time … not just in daydreams I have been making up in one of my splintered aspects of self. The ultimate manifestation of loving-kindness is to experience it both within yourself and also see it in your reality … literally.

That is the power of love. The power of healing. The power of self-actualization and freedom. That is what the spirit of Christmas is all about. Love without conditions is the gift that never stops giving.

It's like waking up to Christmas morning every damn day.

Holiday Bruises by John Caviness

wide awake, not just first thing for presents
but rather since yesterday
even on an eve evils are acted on

stumble down, not the stairs groggily
but instead out of bed
dragging a shell soured by their creator

open up, not just first thing for presents
but to clean a blackened spot
concealed in pajamas to play merry

Untitled 3 by Audrey Barcio

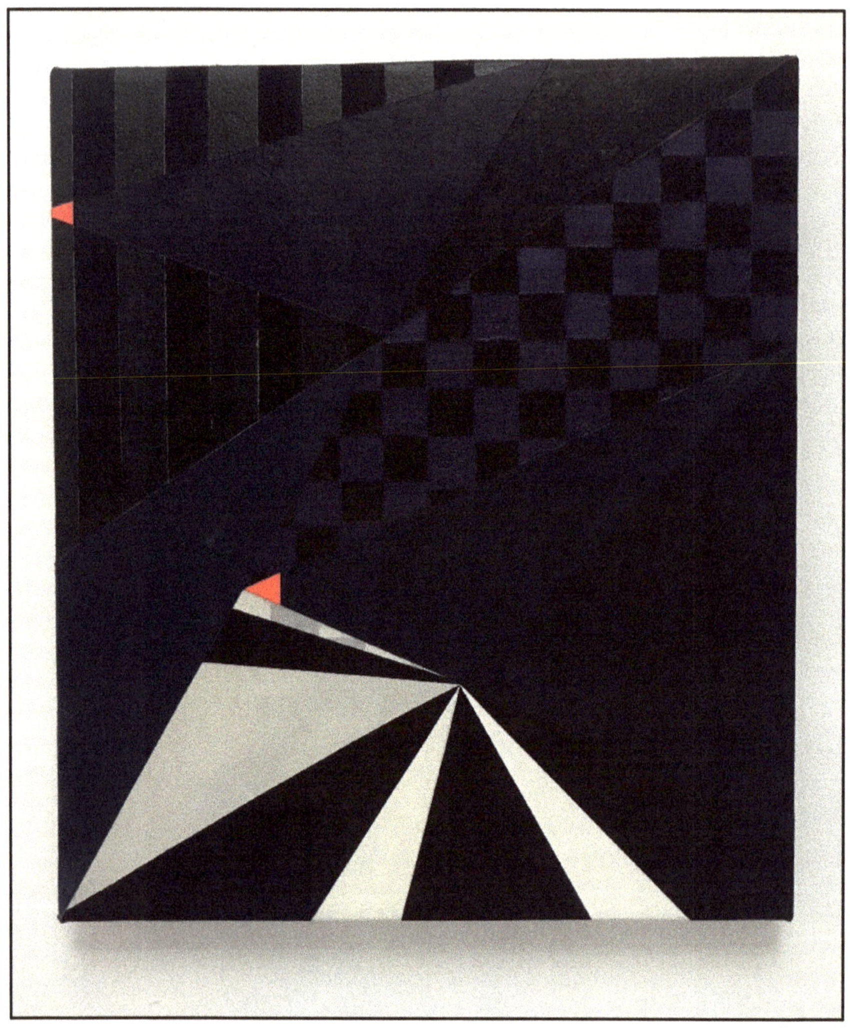

The Poems have Opened Wide their Margins by Jenny Kalahar

The poems have opened wide their margins,
stray words falling everywhere messily, beautifully,
because I love you.
And fountain pens have leaked,
writing their own poems to our love,
heating our cheeks with the embarrassment
of being found out.

A volcano was dormant, but now detonates
in red lava and dangerous rock projectiles
because I love you
and you love me,
and takes no heed of rain falling
or silly arguments that never last because
I love
and you love.
And though a moody raven soars above, shouting warnings,
we will tune him out and listen to sweeter calls
from more colorful birds
that are shaped at a distance like hearts,
imagining that it is always and ever springtime,
even when the grass is covered over for this while.

All around us as we walk here, arm in arm,
I want you only to hear my laughter
and my voice reading poems to you,
shouting over the roar of sun-kissed waterfalls,
or the scrape of leaf-whipped winds,
or the familiarity of our dog barking,
all noises of joy competing with these words,
this poem,
sounding wild and happy and crazy,
because I love you;
because you love me.

Garfield Park Cyanotype by Andrea Haydon

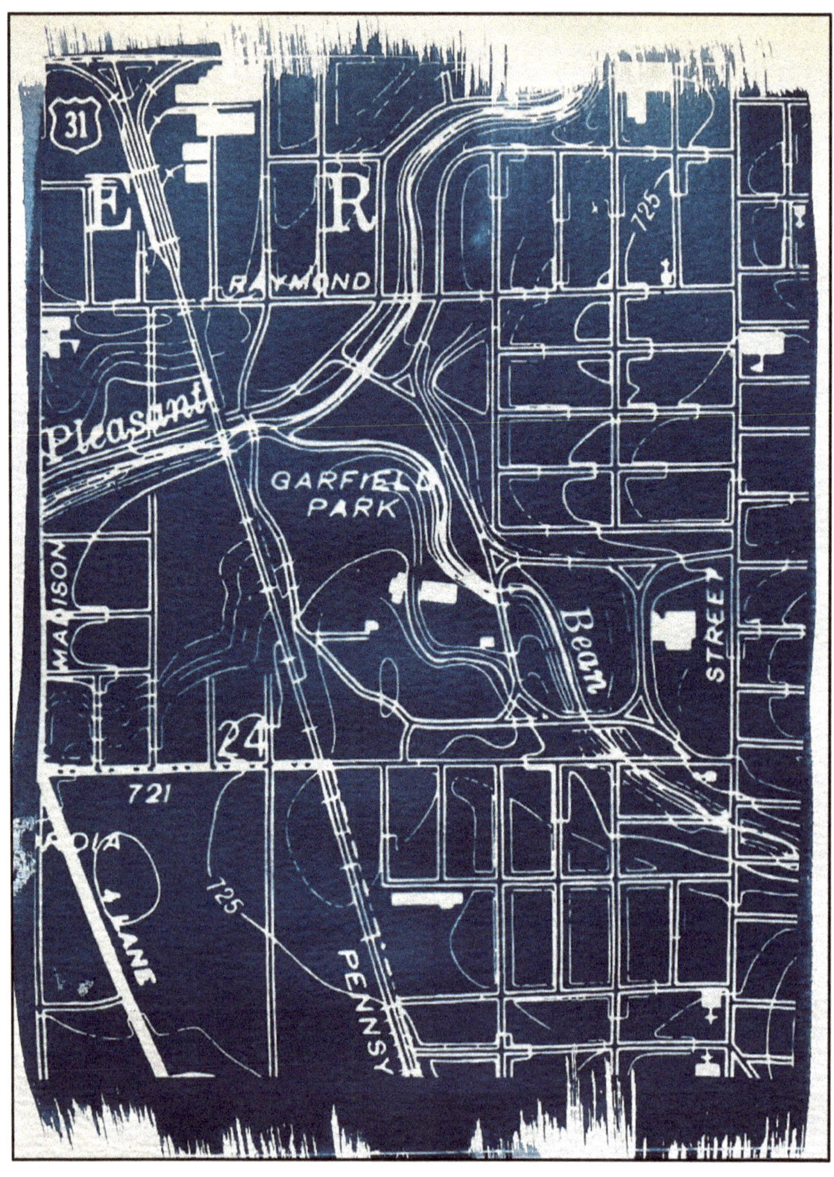

A Voice from Death by John Caviness

hushed, the sound can be heard
passing through the fog, revealing
a wavering woman, to most blurred

cold, the grip of that verisimilitude
shouldering a burden, unwilling
a thankless task, to exude

returned, from Le Grand Mort
delivering a message, divulging
a doomed soul, to immure

We Are Family by George W. Wolfe

Skin color didn't matter. Neither did religion or tribe. The only creed was belief in the team. If you were a Pirates fan, you were family. That was Willie Stargell's idea in 1979, the year Pittsburgh won the World Series.

My buddy Dave and I drove three hours to watch the Bucs play the Phillies at home. Chuck Tanner was the manager. He always remembered my Dad who offered him his first business contract in the 1958 off-season. That was back when big league ball players had to have real jobs in the winter. Tanner had started a school photography business. My dad, a school principal, hired Tanner and his crew to preserve some grade-school memories.

Tanner had burst onto the major league scene in the early 1950s when, playing for the Milwaukee Braves, he hit a home run on the first pitch of his very first time at bat. I still have the baseball he gave me in 1959, signed by all the players on the Cleveland Indians.

Baseball was still in its innocence then, before money corrupted the game, before Pete Rose knew how to gamble, before drugs slid under the table, when Mickey Mantle and Roger Maris were still chasing Babe Ruth's home run record.

Before the game all I wanted was to get a message to Tanner. I never thought I'd have a chance. But to our surprise, he invited us into the locker room. All I had to say was my dad's name. It was magical. The receptionist in the park office called down to say, "Harold Wolfe's son is here." In an instant the beloved manager, with his infectious smile, welcomed us into his office where he signed a baseball. *To my friend Harold. Chuck Tanner.*

During the game, things got heated. I choked on my beer when the umpire made a terrible call at first base. The crowd rose to its feet as Tanner charged onto the field and gave the ump a face-full.

"We are family" had become the rallying cry for Pirate fans. The pop group *Sister Sledge* hit one out of the park that summer with their song by the same name, and by August, everyone in Pittsburgh knew the words. Watching Stargell get mobbed at home after hitting the winning home run in the 14th inning was the only steroid anyone needed.

That day, Three Rivers Stadium felt like home.

Grocery Days by Alys Caviness-Gober

In the old days, grocery shopping took my husband about an hour. Nowadays, it takes two to three hours, because of lines and limits to how many people can be in stores at one time, and, of course, going to multiple stores.

I'm two rooms away from the kitchen when he returns from grocery shopping; as always nowadays, he wears a mask and gloves.

I stay where I am.

In "the old days," I'd have jumped up to help put away groceries.

He knows I'm going to stay where I am, but he still shouts at me through his mask to

"STAY AWAY!"

and I shout back, "OKAY!"

I hear the kitchen door open and close a few times as he brings in our treasures (nowadays, anything and everything he brings home is a treasure to me).

I hear him, back in the kitchen, in punctuated sounds.

Opening and closing the kitchen door, and I know he's wiped down the door handles, to keep me safe.

Silence, with intermittent slight noises, and I know he's thoroughly wiping down every item he purchased, to keep me safe.

Refrigerator door opening and closing, and I know he's putting away perishables, all wiped-down to keep me safe.

Back porch door opening and closing, and I know he's putting some wiped-down non-perishables out there for a while, for extra "let the virus die" time, before putting them in the pantry, to keep me safe.

I hear the washing machine start; I know he's put his clothes in there, to keep me safe.

Down the hall, I hear the shower start; I know he's washing away potential virus particles, to keep me safe.

That all takes about an hour or so, then he shouts, "YOU CAN BE IN THE KITCHEN"

and I shout, "I LOVE YOU"

and he shouts, "I LOVE YOU BACK."

I wait a minute, working to regain control enough that my tears dry up, then I go into the kitchen.

We stand across the room from each other, and I smile and wave at him.

He grins and waves back.

Cris (St. George's Island 2016) by Alys Caviness-Gober

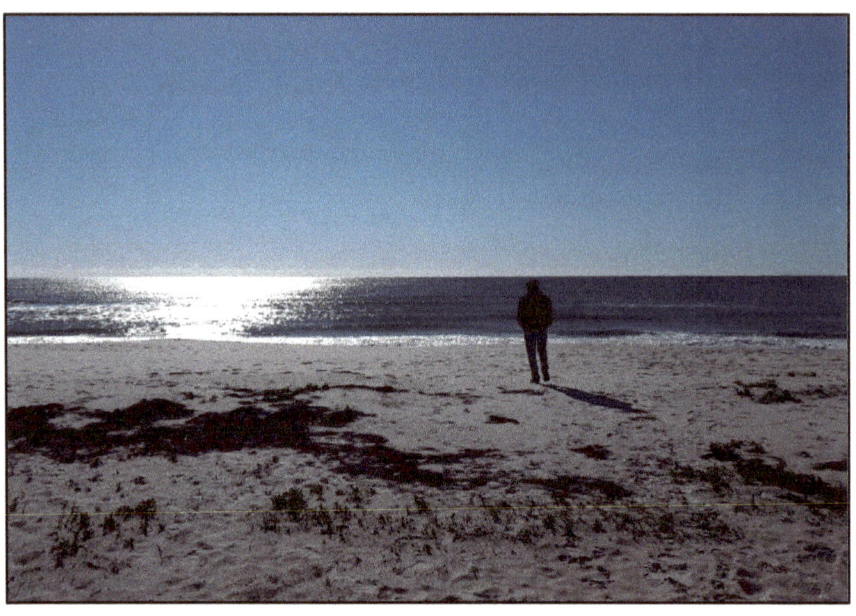

If walls could talk? by John Caviness

Chipped paint observers
Seeing the past and present as one
Witnesses to what you want the world to see
And plenty you wouldn't

Trapped reverberated voices
Long since spoken or recently shouted
Audience to sounds you want the world to hear
And plenty you wouldn't

Stomps, slams, accidental or otherwise
Felt throughout the inner workings of those walls
Victims of your anger and frustrated mistakes
And plenty they could say

But never will

Alcohol Ink Mugs by Andrea Haydon

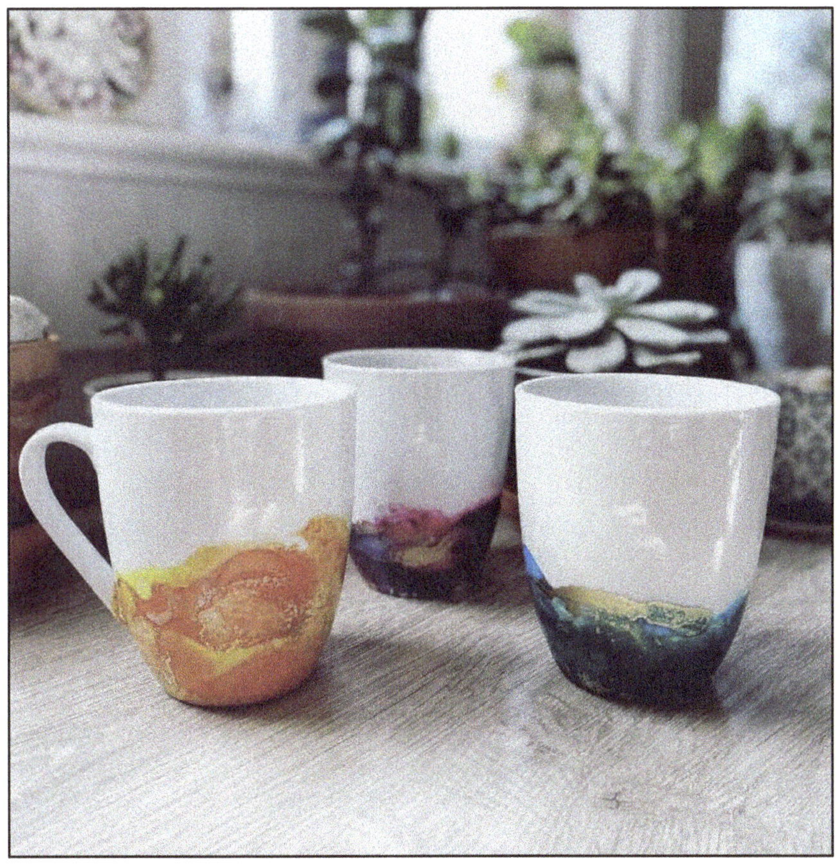

Holding Your Grandchildren: The Candle Burns Quickly by George Wylie

With the tiniest of hands and roundest of faces, they lure you in,
drawing you close to feel the warmth of their heads, see the lift of their smiles,
touch the wisps of their hair, enhance your own value by their dependence.
You are soberly aware of the shortness of their time needing you.
Hold them close: the candle of time burns quickly.

With bright eyes following you they share this new world of yours,
which they deserve the best of but is bestowed to them soiled.

The tiny hands grip your finger and the doll-like feet jump about.
You bring your best and warmest game, your graceful kindness.
Hold them close: the candle of time burns quickly.

A face of purity, a mouth of smiles, the eyes are chocked with trust.
Holding them mines out what is left of your purity; and you try to pass it to them.
You deign to shore yourself up with their reliance.
You try to absorb some of the soft pinkness of them onto yourself.
Hold them close: the candle of time burns quickly.

Before the grandchildren came, you were unaware there was a hole to fill.
They are the new proof there was some reason you grew their parents.
The love you bequeath them will not be in the genes, but soaked up in the hands of their grandparents.
Look into their eyes, give unabashed approval, stream love at them even if you reach somewhere for it.
Hold them close: the candle of time burns quickly.

Biting by John Caviness

Is a pinched point
the source of annoyances,
or resultant joy?

Dust by Jenny Kalahar

Leaning against the white-worn barn
that had only housed tools
and a four-door sedan my whole childhood
but still smelled of the long-dead family cow on damp days,
I watched the empty field across the empty road
before or after crops had come or left
as wisps of wind
shaped whirls of rustbrown dust
into figures I was sure I recognized.
They would not swirl together
as if the dust figures, like memories, had sworn

never to occupy the same space at the same time.

A gathering of blackbirds held a meeting
along the dipping metal fence
as if their weight or repeated landings there
had sloped it over time,
shouting disagreements
ruffling feathers at each other
each knowing they were right
about what they were seeing in the rising dust.
I listened, realizing how wrong I was:
That plume of debris was not my mother over the stove
waving me closer to test for saltiness from her spoon,
and the next was not the banana-seat bicycle
that had rolled me over
the crisscrossing streets of my small hometown,
nor was the next image an infant in my husband's arms,
his fat tears falling, falling
into the maelstrom of a sudden death.
No. The birds were closer to the truth
and I had fooled myself again.
I turned to enter the barn for a hammer
more intent on smashing delusions
than I had ever been before.

Flaming New Year by Vivianne Belle
(adapted from a cocktail by bartender Yael Vengroff)

Ingredients:

- 3/4 ounce lime juice, freshly squeezed
- 1/3 ounce simple syrup
- 4 – 6 basil leaves
- 1.5 – 2 ounces whiskey of your choice
- 1/2 ounce Campari (or bitters of your choice)
- Crushed ice
- Optional: 1 sugar cube for flaming lime shell

Steps:

- Add lime juice, syrup, and basil leaves together in a glass and press gently with a muddler.
- Add whiskey and crushed ice.

- Float Campari on top and more crushed ice.
- Optional: garnish with a flaming lime shell: squeeze juice from half a lime into a small dish. Place lime shell atop prepared cocktail and place 1 sugar cube inside. Douse sugar cube with whiskey and carefully light on fire. Extinguish & remove before drinking cocktail.

Flaming Irish New Year Image: from Liquor.com / Tim Nusog

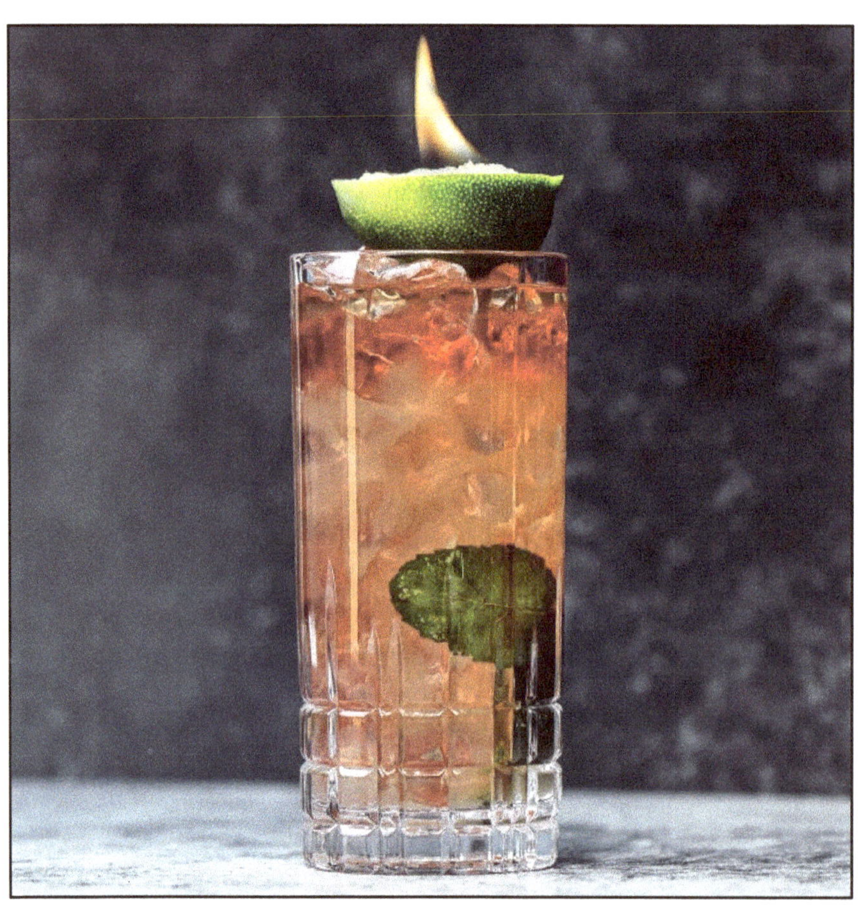

Dark (K)night by John Caviness

Sundered dark
In the eve
Left alone
After hours

Through fog
Dishonored stride
Armor broken
After sunrise

You Should Have Thought Of That by Lori Hand

Me: *Hello, this is Lori Hand, and I'm a patient of Dr. Cline. I'm calling because I just got a positive pregnancy test.*
Nurse: *Oh, okay, congratulations? What was the date of your last normal menstrual period?*
Me: *It was March 19.*
Nurse: *Let's see. That makes your due date ... December 24.*
Me: *Oh no, really? I always hated my December birthday. My mom is gonna laugh her ass off.*
Nurse: *Well. You should have thought of that.*

What a thing to say to an obsessive overthinker. Yes, of course I should have thought of that. I was 36 and had endured 15 consecutive months of disappointment, and all those invasive and painful tests and procedures, after already delaying thoughts of having a family – because who brings a child into a post-9/11 world? But I guess I should have just not tried that one month (which, as it happens, was the only month in my life that I was able to get pregnant)?

I flashed back, as I often still do, to a childhood birthday. I was already jealous enough of my next-door neighbor, who always had cake and ice cream and games at her early-July outdoor fetes. Our house was not large and my father was not tolerant of chaos. So a December birthday party with anyone but family was usually out of the question. One year mom got a store-bought cake. I leaned over to peek through the cellophane lid, and there it was, covered in red poinsettias: "Happy Birthday Lori and Kelli." Ah yes, there was that other complication. Four years and three days after I was born, I got a sister.

Thus began a long history of trying to protect my birthday from everything else happening at the same time. More than once I heard, "Now this is a big present, so it's for your birthday AND Christmas." And sometimes people had the "audacity" to wrap my birthday present in Christmas paper.

When Christmas Eve did arrive those many years later, I actually defied the odds and went into labor on my due date. As the clock inched toward midnight and my labor failed to progress, the doctor returned from Christmas Eve church services and asked me how I'd feel about a C-section.

"Can you have her out before midnight?" I asked. He nodded. "Okay, go for it," I agreed.

At 10:39pm, Cate made her debut, while our extended family, who had driven in from a 4-hour radius in all directions, watched *A Christmas Story* on the waiting-room TV more times than they could count. I had saved her from the world's worst birthdate, but just barely.

Now my mission shifted from protecting my birthday to protecting hers. I admit I don't always do a good job of maintaining birthday intent when buying presents, and often find myself flipping a mental coin about which wrapping paper a particular gift will get. But we have always made a point to get her an ice cream cake, with no poinsettias, and with "Happy Birthday Cate" specially written on it. I've organized bounce-house parties, ice-skating-parties, and indoor pool parties (earlier in the month, so that people could attend). I once threw a half-birthday extravaganza in the backyard in June, but it was of course all but forgotten by the time Christmas Eve rolled around again.

Sometimes the stress is too much and I forget my manners. My favorite joke though the years was always when she'd ask for something she'd see on TV. "Put it on your Christmas list," I would say. "But that's not soon enough!" she would inevitably cry. "Oh, okay," I'd say, "Put it on your birthday list." (LOL. It never gets old.)

Now here we are just days from her 17th birthday, in the midst of a global pandemic, and I'm recovering from another major surgery. I thought ahead and started ordering her DQ cake online, which we could pick up at the drive-through instead of going inside and picking out something from the freezer like we always do. Surprisingly, I found her resistant when I tried to choose a more birthday-oriented design. "No, I want the one with penguins," she said. A few years prior we'd ended up with penguins when the other choices weren't good. As it turns out, penguins are a tradition in her mind, and she sees them as more "winter" than "Christmas." I guess I've been trying too hard. Penguins through the drive-through, it is.

She is particularly upset about the inability to spend time with friends on her actual birthday. It's always been difficult to find friends who could spare time from their families on Christmas Eve. But this year the chance of letting a friend into our house is less than zero. I feel awful that this is how she will remember high school. For the most part she gets it, but it still hurts. I sometimes still wonder whether I made the right decision to start a family when I did. I mean, could I have predicted how bad things would be by now? *Should* I have thought of that?

A cousin gave me a wall hanging for her birth that read, "A baby is God's opinion that the world should go on." And I guess I did think of that – of everything – and decided to choose hope. A Christmas Eve birthday is super magical (in my reformed opinion). I honestly believe that one day we'll be able to do the things we used to do and see the people we want to see. So that's what I choose to think of: hope.

Blue Eyes by John Caviness

Like the ocean
deep blues mixed with greens
I've been lost in them
and others lost in mine

Royal Crown by Sandra Natais

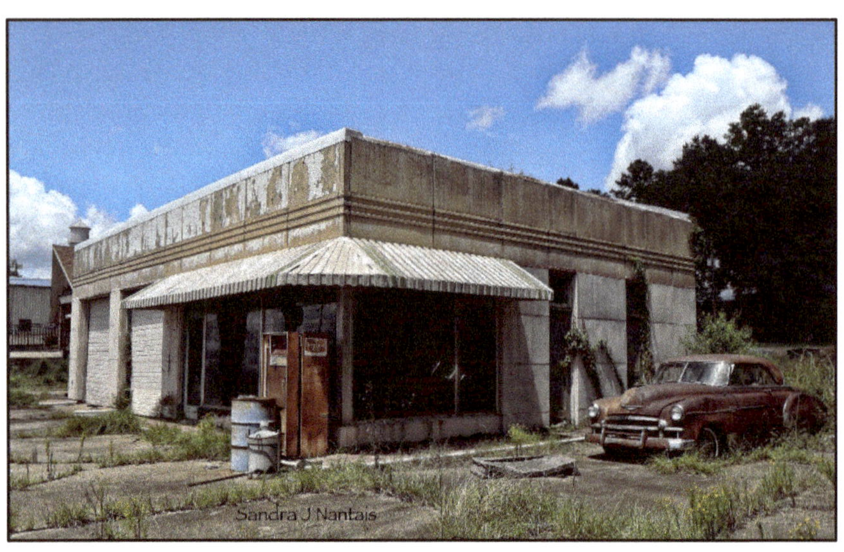

Royal Crown by Michael E. Strosahl

I hear there is a marker
and a plot to hold his bones,
not three miles away
from where he spent
summers working for dad,
pumping fuel and
washing windows

until the day
they raised Royal Crown
to a nickel in the machine
and Daddy's ticker
couldn't take it anymore.

They say he struggled
to fill his father's shoes.
Instead of seeing the world,
he worked the garage,
wore a path bare
through the grass and
up to his Daddy's stone

for chats, advice.
Kept the old man's Chevy
running smooth,
but never took her out on the road.

Legend has it
he never left a stranded traveler,
never failed to pop the cap
of a twelve ounce bottle
on the counter's edge
just to see a kid smile.

I'm told he shuttered the shop in the 80s.
In the 90s he pulled the pumps,
moved himself into the back,
tinkering on an occasional carburetor,
cleaning up two bays never used.

I read in the paper
he'd been dead
near two weeks when found,
heart seized
like a motor run out of oil,
laid back in his La-Z-Boy,
half a bottle of RC
gone flat on the table nearby.

I thought of him
just the other day
as I drove by the old station,
still empty,
his Daddy's Chevy
rusted into the space he left it,
the machine that shared
iced Royal Crown
faded dark and empty
the day he passed.
I haven't had a cold one since.

Brought Back by John Caviness

molded by the hands of strangers
hefted and heaved into a pile
stood a spirit vacationing
on a cold winter day

balled up with limbs unfamiliar
the golem saw once more what life was
encompassed by lodges all so similar
it began to remember, over a wick alive

some time ago, he had a name
a little lodge of his own
surrounded by more of the same
good thoughts and cider on loan

brought back to time now present
the monster wandered, passing each door
a wreath of thoughts attacking his mind
he took to paper, but ran out of time

What is Family Anyway by George Wylie

What is a family anyway, you ask, knowing already how you perceive it,
but wondering if I will somehow deconstruct it.
But before I commit to pedantics, I'll check my dictionary.
"A social unit consisting of parents and their children."
There, simple enough.

So without bringing in sweet violins and baby coos, I'll try to do mine justice.
I see Mom's haste turn to a smile as she tucked me in, treating all of us as special.
I see her pride as we stood in church to read a reluctantly mumbled verse
Or returning dirty from scout camp with oak leaves in our clothes.

I see Dad grimace when we weren't polite but smile when we were generous.
And his apparent vow to never once call us names or curse us.
I remember his hug, held a bit longer when I boarded a plane in uniform,
And a small tear when I tendered over our first cotton-wrapped child to his lap.

I slept under a white Bates bedspread, protected by Roy Rogers on the wall.
On our knees we always recited the same bedtime prayer, more for her than Him.
Four boys and a girl, we were generously obnoxious and always in trouble.
The worst bedtime words were Dad's, "*AM I GOING TO HAVE TO COME UP THERE?*"

As much as we bickered, we were fiercely loyal if someone attacked a sib.
As much as I often hated my brother, I was fast to strike someone who pushed him.
But I see all-day roasting beef with green beans, a dessert pie, and a hug.
I see a litter of kittens and hear Dad's phony threats to take them away.

There is so much more to family than this ditty. At best it greets a newborn child
And at worst it closes a flowered casket on a done-blooming life.
It celebrates unity, thickens our blood, and thins the miles and the years apart.
Family rewards tolerance and perpetuates loyalty. It plugs us in.

Winter Rain by Alys Caviness-Gober

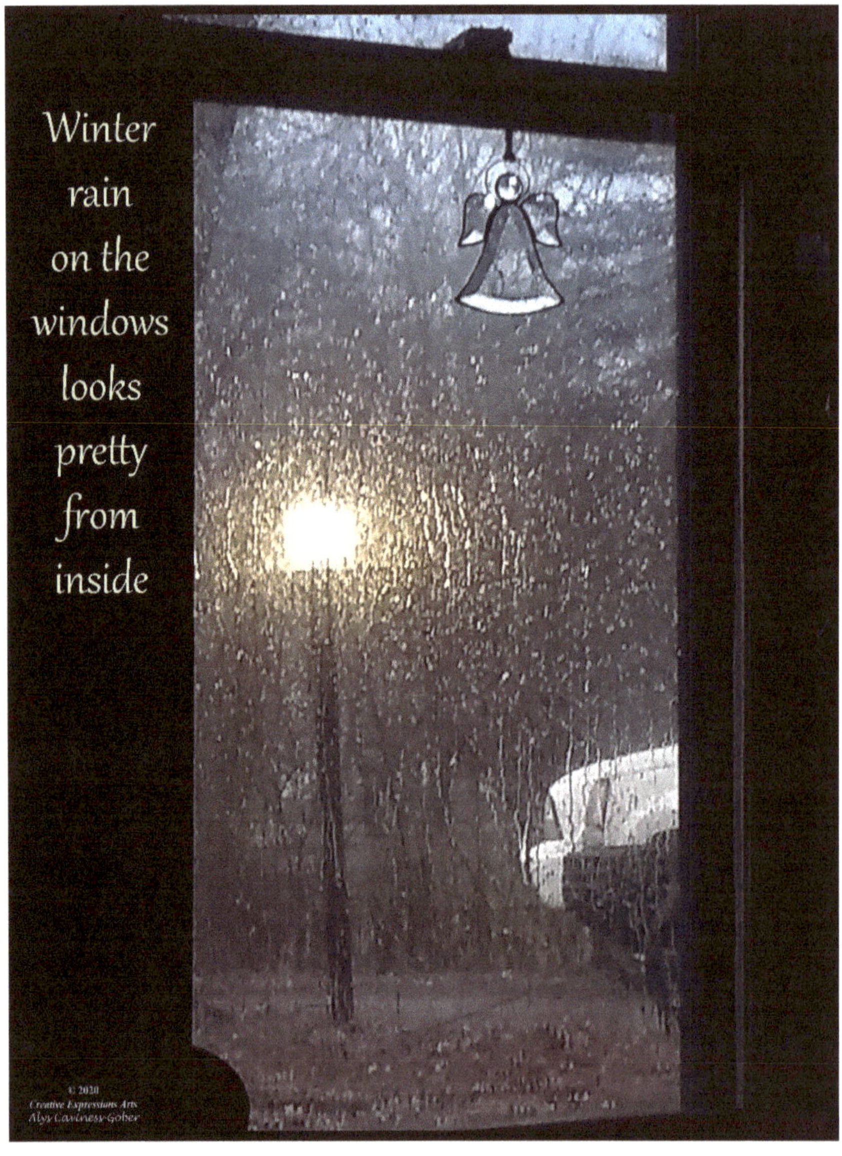

Tin by Jenny Kalahar

Church was a tin chapel,
cold on gray mornings,
a sweatbox in summer,
all uncomfortable,
dressed for a funeral
in shiny shoes, black
over white socks.
Carpeting to muffle any joyful tap,
padded pews to cushion my agony.

Church for me was a tin chapel.
Words from the front a blur of noise,
my ears perking up when the organ played,
when I could hum along before I could read the hymnal
or sing along badly.
The hymns were my heartfelt prayers
as I stared at the stained-glass lambs
and folded and refolded my mother's bulletin,
aching at the end when the organ echoed and died,
skipping free when the candles were snuffed, and we were released.

Church was a tin chapel
suffocating sobersides with somber expressions.
I wanted to take a can opener to the top
to let in air and sun and the purer rays of Jesus's love
that these familiar, dull faces just weren't appreciating,
sitting stiffly in suits and skirts and white shirts,
listening more to their own worries than sermons,
paying their dues to God who wouldn't want such formalities
from his children every Sunday.

Habits of Frost by John Caviness

Dreams of returning to the forest
stretching a sheet across cooling lands
lying upon branches and the rocks
streams of unmoving water beneath.

Brittle to the touch
even the most gentle footfall fractures
encased life, sleeping, waiting
for the habits of sunshine.

Winter Scene by Andrea Haydon

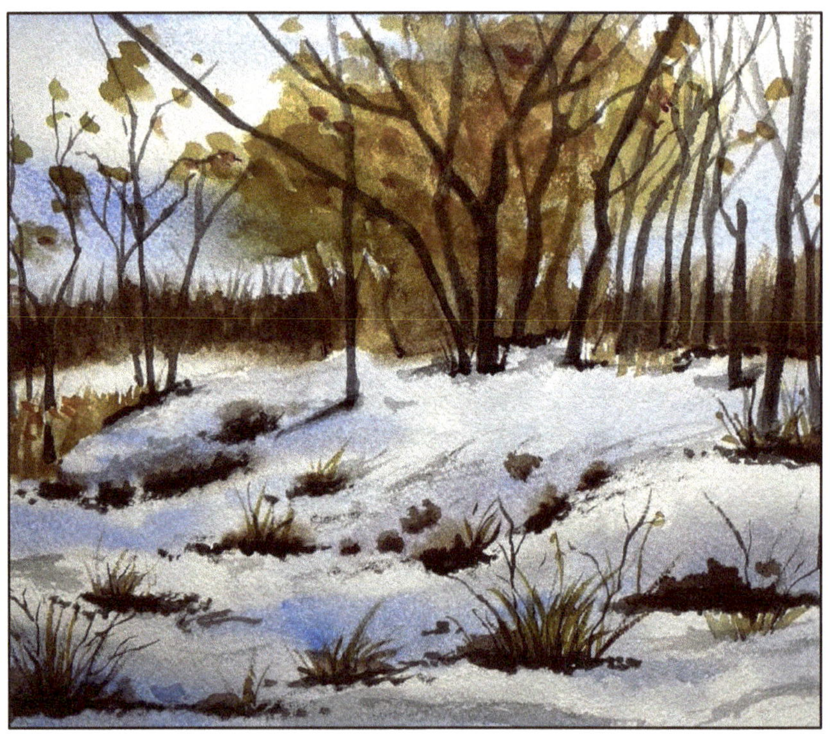

The Crepe Myrtle by Michael E. Strosahl

Her eyes fell,
for that matter
her whole soul drooped
for reasons she would not say,

but we knew it was Spanish Moss
that blurred her days,
obscuring even the moon
as it shone down

upon those lonely nights
where only the occasional dream
held the bloom

of younger years
and those bright eyes,
that beautiful smile
still aglow in the memory
of an evening spent
under the Crepe Myrtle,
a place she never felt alone.

Untitled by John Caviness

coughing, high above
sick and snowbound
all could hear the Carol of hells
a candy cane curse from shadows below
each freckled with light
choking, on chimney fumes

Rites of Passage by Patrick Kalahar

Because of a slight injury, I'm sitting alone in one of the recently built basic training barracks of Fort Benning, Georgia, while the rest of my company of recruits are still training in the field. I think of red dust and red mud. The taste of it. The smell of it. The grit of it in my teeth, in my eyes, under my fingernails and between my toes. I also smell fresh white paint and see a ghostly image bleeding faintly through the paint – the letters O-H-I-O. I wonder if the letters were painted by a homesick soldier from Ohio. I know the feeling. I miss my home on a farm south of Royalton, Indiana, and my family, friends, and a dog named Zip I'd raised from a puppy. He's old now. God, I doubt I'll ever see that dog again.

I think of what the future holds and the coming war. Are the red pools of Fort Benning mud foretelling pools of blood for me and the rest of us in basic training? Are we headed for Europe or Asia?

The drill sergeants tell us (it seems like fifty times a day) that the United States will officially enter the war in a matter of weeks or even days. They yell and scream at us and shove our faces into the mud with steel-toed boots while we squeeze under barbed-wire, saying we are not crawling low enough. They kick us when we are too slow following an order because we are exhausted, and punch crybabies in the face with hard fists that sting and shame.

At first, I hated the drill sergeants – and I never really hated anybody in my whole life. But the old timers, guys who were in the Army before, got out, and enlisted again, and the lifers who were not drill sergeants, told us the drills were not really bad guys. They were mostly married and had families. But they had served in the Great War … and they remembered.

They remembered that thousands of our boys died needlessly. The drills were the survivors. Most had children old enough to fight in this new war and they said, "never again." Never again would they allow young men to go to war untrained and soft. The drills would make them hard – hard as seasoned oak. If that meant being mean and cruel now but giving recruits a chance at a long life with children and grandchildren of their own, then that was worth the price.

As I sit alone in the barracks and consider the future, my thoughts keep returning to the past. I feel very young in this moment, and in danger of fading away; lost and forgotten in the present terrors unless I grasp and hold tightly to every memory …

It is the summer of 1933, and I am eleven years old. My dog and I are walking down the main street of Royalton, a small village surrounded by farms, including the one I live on. On the main street and the square formed around it are the courthouse (the biggest building in the whole county), the old jail, and nearly all the businesses. There are more horses and wagons than cars, and some of the stores are closed and boarded because of the Depression. Each store window has the same small patriotic N-R-A poster in the window – even the closed stores. I don't know exactly what it means, but I hear my father and other men say it means "Recovery." Inside every open business is a portrait that says, *Our New President – Franklin Delano Roosevelt*. "He is going to save the country," I hear the adults say.

Even Republicans.

My father writes stories for the weekly newspaper, and he and my mother and me (and Zip, of course) live on my grandparents' farm. We're in town to buy supplies for the big Connaught family reunion. The whole extended Connaught family comes each summer from all over the country for the celebration. For a lot of them, in these Depression years, it is the only thing they spend money on that is not an absolute necessity.

Last year, a strange old man, very thin and shy, came all the way from the west coast of Ireland. He was one of my grandfather's uncles, and he was a priest. My father said, "He speaks mostly Gaelic, some English, and enough Latin to say the mass and read from the Bible and prayerbook." He constantly smoked cigarettes that he rolled himself, and drank Irish whiskey neat, poured – when anybody offered – into a shot glass that he kept in the pocket of his clerical jacket.

Zip and I dozed peacefully on the trip back from town to the farm, then spent the rest of the day and evening doing chores for whoever asked – whenever they could find us. We stayed hidden as much as possible.

The big day dawned, and the whole farm was bustling. The farmhouse and barn were packed with close relatives, and the fields were filled with tents. The rich people – relatively speaking – stayed in boarding houses or hotels in Indianapolis or drove their cars all night or early in the morning. My family arranged for the tables and chairs and everything, and they and those living the closest supplied most of the food. The women and my father and grandfather were up well before dawn preparing the food and refreshments, and the men slaughtered a pig and chickens for the big, open fire roast. Pretty much all the men brought their own whiskey! The whole crowd – except some of the in-laws – was Irish, after all.

No one ever seemed to know who started it, but a few men always passed the hat, and everything from dimes to twenty-dollar bills were dropped in while all eyes turned skyward, taking great interest in the trees and clouds.

There were games and loud and raucous conversations, punctuated with flailing arms and jabbing fingers; lewd and vulgar jokes (some anti-clerical as only the Irish, that most Catholic of people, could tell them), accompanied by almost hysterical laughter "like the din of Bedlam," as my Aunt May (who was a retired nun) would often say. These stories and jokes were always permitted because they were told with such charm and dancing eyes that none could take offence. I rarely took part directly in any of the activities, content to listen and observe.

There were two men that I'd particularly noticed all through the morning. They were clearly not relatives or a part of the happy throng. They shook hands and talked with many of the men, but never when any women were around. Their gestures were secretive, and their smiles were tight and thin-lipped and never reached their darting eyes.

I moved as close as I dared to listen and watch what was going on. The relatives all knew who I was and took no notice. The two strangers did notice, but clearly sized me up as no threat. I was eleven years old, after all. They were talking Irish politics, and I heard things like Sinn Fein and IRA and Provos and death to all the Black and Tans and the collaborators who were still in Ireland. Then one of my relatives looked around and handed one of the strangers a huge wad of money, and he put it in an inside pocket of his suit. When he did so, I was almost sure I saw a gun in a shoulder-holster. I acted like I was totally bored, kicked at a couple of rocks, and as casually as I could I walked away, pretending to look for something more interesting.

Just when I thought my encounter with the IRA was going to be the highlight of the reunion – if they didn't kill me, that is – I literally bumped into a girl who was about my age and very pretty. I'd seen her a number of times through the morning, and every time she looked in my direction, I was sure she smiled. But each time I quickly looked away, convinced she was looking at someone else or that she smiled at everyone. I was very shy.

Well, now I could hardly ignore her. I apologized and started to turn away, but the girl smiled and put out her hand and said, "Hi. My name is Francine, but everybody, except my teachers, calls me Fran or Franny. I'm not a relative. I'm just here with one of my school friends and her family. They're distant cousins of yours or something." All this just tumbled out in a second or two. Before I could even think of what to say, she added, "I already know your name is Aidan Connaught and that you're eleven."

"Almost twelve – in less than a month," I interrupted.

"Well, Aidan Connaught, almost twelve in less than a month, I am twelve, almost thirteen in a little over a month. But I don't think that really matters, do you? A boy can like an older woman if he wants."

I had to laugh, and then we laughed together. It was the first time ever that I was at ease talking to a girl. We entered every race and contest we could. The three-legged sack race, the egg-balancing on a spoon race, the egg roll race, the from here to over there on the other side of the field race, and other games, too.

I, who never took part and just wanted to observe, was taking part in every event that came along. We talked nonstop, and in no time, we were holding hands. We walked to the river that was about a half mile from where the reunion was set up. We laughed about whatever came into our heads. Suddenly Fran said, "Let's go swimming!"

I swallowed hard and said, "I didn't bring a swimming suit."

She said, "I've got mine on under my clothes. My friend said she was sure there was somewhere to swim on the farm, so I came prepared. But you could just take off your shirt and go in like that … or take off your shorts, too, if you don't want to wear them around wet. Just go in the water in your underwear. No one is close enough to see that they are not swimming trunks." Then Fran gave me a mischievous smile and said, "Or just go skinny-dipping. My brothers do it all the time. Nobody cares if boys do it. I would do it myself if I could."

My face heated up, and I know I turned bright red. I couldn't tell her that I'd never been skinny-dipping in my life. Not even when I was swimming all alone.

She quickly stripped off her clothes and mock posed in her one-piece skintight swimsuit that she proudly said was made of "Rayon Satin

Lastex." I stripped to my underwear and ran quickly into the water with Fran close behind me, laughing and screeching at the first blast of cool water after being overheated all day.

"I must say, Mr. Connaught, you didn't cut a very elegant figure running into the river with one hand gripping your underwear," Fran drawled Hollywood style.

I gave her the biggest splash possible, and she squealed and sputtered. "Oh, I'm going to get you good for that!" she said in mock anger as she dove toward me head-first. For a fleeting moment, all I saw was her rear and legs, and then she was gone. Time seemed to stop as I wondered where she went. Then I felt her head ram me in the stomach and her hands grab me around the waist. She yanked my briefs down below my knees, then burst out of the water right in front of me, laughing and spitting water. I was angry and terribly embarrassed, but I looked at Fran and what I saw in her smile and bright, dancing eyes was pure joy, touched with sly mischief, and I felt something that I knew I'd never felt before. All I knew for certain was it sure wasn't anger.

I stood there for probably a few seconds – though it seemed like forever – and then leaned down and pulled up my underwear. I didn't know what to say or do, but Fran broke the tension and said, "Don't worry. I always keep my eyes closed when I swim underwater." She gave me another playful splash and swam to the other side of the river, and I followed. We spent another short while laughing and playing water tag, and then we decided that we had better get back to the reunion. It was time to eat, anyway.

The two of us swam to the riverbank where we'd left our clothes. Fran said, "Let's go into the trees by that big rock to get dressed. You should take off your wet underwear and wring them out before putting them back on or they will soak through your new shorts and be very uncomfortable. I'm going to take off my swimsuit and put on my clothes without it. We can stand facing away from each other while we get dressed. That way we can also see if anybody is coming from either direction along the river." She hesitated, then added, "Promise me you won't turn around." I promised, but there was something in her voice that made me unsure if it was a demand or a challenge. I was very aware that we were both naked only a few feet apart, but I dutifully kept my promise. I didn't know if she kept the same promise, but I was shocked to realize I didn't care if she didn't.

It was all very innocent and sweet. I was not quite twelve and Fran was not quite thirteen, but I felt different. I knew everything had changed forever, and I felt happy but also very sad for something I knew I had lost.

Then I knew why – sitting alone in the barracks – I was thinking so much about that particular reunion. It was a moment in time very like that summer day at the Connaught reunion in 1933. I was dreaming of the past and regretting a certain lost innocence. Then, and again now, I was facing a frightening but necessary future. The past is a closed book – already written – but the future is still to be created. Innocence is overtaken by experience. There is no other way.

Two Brothers by Steve VandeWater
(song lyric)

My Grampa was a bootlegger in nineteen twenty-five
In Prohibition that was how a lot of folks survived
The government said no more booze, but my Grampa had other views
And soon he found a novel way to make his business thrive

His older brother Larry graduated seminary
And soon became the pastor at a little local church
They needed sacramental wine and that was right up Grampa's line
So Father Larry didn't have too very far to search

America was getting thirsty. Couldn't get a legal drink
But ev'ry Sunday Catholics could get a little sip
The Mass became more popular than ever it had been before
Some Baptists even snuck in for to take a little nip

With all those people in the pew, it's funny no one ever knew
The washtub wine that they adored was really bathtub gin
It was mostly just grain alcohol, watered down, but that ain't all
For flavor and for coloring he splashed some grape juice in

As the church's small attendance soared, results just couldn't be ignored
The flock had grown in numbers that no one could quite explain
The Pope in Rome asked Larry please, to run the whole Archdiocese
And Grampa Harry's enterprise seemed almost preordained

With all those churches to supply my Grampa's still would soon run dry
He grew the operation to include a dozen more
Demand was growing bigger and my Grampa Harry figured
That a future as a millionaire was what he had in store

Things went well 'til thirty-four, but only just a month before
They voted Prohibition out and church attendance dropped
Now folks could get wine anywhere and pews again were nearly bare
And Grampa's stills grew stiller until finally they stopped

Archbishop Larry fared no better. Pretty soon he got a letter
Relocating him to somewhere out along the coast
They found he could not duplicate receipts in his collection plate
So Larry got demoted to a less important post

Two brothers' fortunes intertwined around that bootleg holy wine
The priest no longer used the stuff to celebrate The Word
The bootlegger retired but his recipe inspired
Brands like Mad Dog 20/20, Night Train Express, and Thunderbird

Rest Stop by John Caviness

frosty fowls make a cold entrance
wishing for a place to recess
to dream of pine and evergreen pockets
hardened icy bowers embrace
on a shivering reprieve of their longing pass

Bull by Andrea Haydon

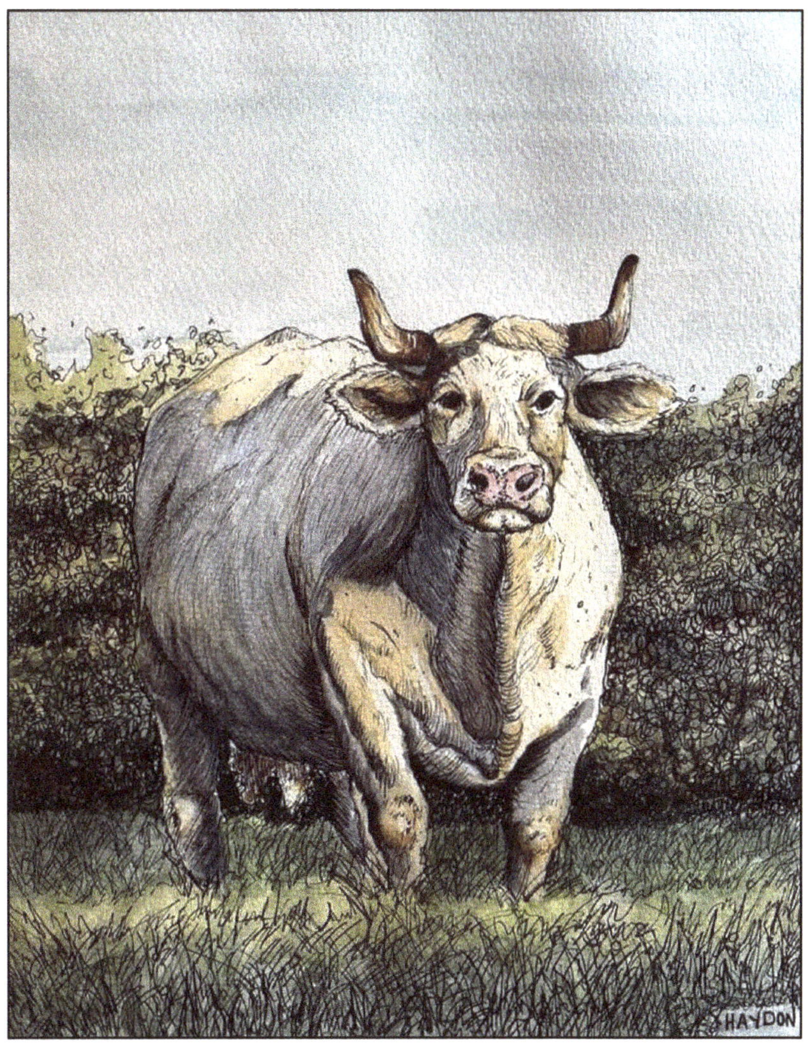

September Harvest by Marlene Million

I remember grandmother's brown brick home,
white, waterfall petunias cascading
over her window boxes, and yellow finch chirps
atop her purple cone flowers.

Fruity, tart aroma drifted from basement area,
as bushels of peaches, apples lined the floor.

Nutmeg and cinnamon whirled from pot's mixture,
as I stirred, soothing my soul with freshness.

I relished the rich blend being ladled
into Ball jars, setting them in a canning rack
for a hot-water bath. Cooled cans were stored
in grandma's cellar, and I awaited spooning
and tasting her lush autumn fare.

Can I Touch Him? by George Wylie

Mom and I kneeled in front of the casket, which held Grandpa in a box with way too much satin. His face had been powdered with something, his hair combed all wrong. And they'd jammed him into a tweed suit. I hadn't seen him in a suit. It looked way too stiff. And Grandpa wasn't grinning. He'd always grinned. The funeral home guys must not have known him. He was so much smaller here, and why'd they made his lips so thin?

Mom was saying a prayer so I tried one too, but it wasn't much. We were surrounded by tons of smelly flowers. Somewhere a speaker was playing an organ song. Grandpa had an old pump organ and they said he played it well, before he went mostly blind. I never knew him then when he could still see, but I did pump away on that organ some and he didn't seem to mind. I was aware of the people behind me watching. My Dad, my cousins, the stiff people from the church.

At first Grandpa seemed plastic but I began to zone in on him and he seemed now warmer. It really was him. I leaned to Mom and said,

"Can I touch Him?"

"No!" she said. *"You can't touch him. Of course not. That isn't right."*

"Mom, I want to touch Grandpa's face just for a minute. I won't hurt him. And I want to give him this."

"Absolutely not," she declared. *"Let's get up now and let other people in here. Come on."*

After we greeted some neighbors, I drew her into a small fancy sitting room with lace doilies.

"Mom, why didn't you let me touch Grandpa?"

"Now you listen to me," she said. *"It isn't proper."*

She was always a bit too much into propriety and manners. I was not always into them.

She began to describe some of the formalities of funeral visitations … and I started to cry.

"And what was that dirty thing you wanted to put in there? You can't just put your stuff in a casket. You're eleven now and need to act like an adult."

"Will you let me say what I want to say, Mom, and don't interrupt me." She stopped and looked at me. *"Mom, the reason I wanted to touch Grandpa is because he always touched me."*

"What?" she said. *"Where did he touch you?"*

"No it wasn't that, Mom. Will you listen to me?"

I was still crying a little and had my back to the door where aunts and church ladies and stuff were passing by, looking in.

"Okay. You know he couldn't see hardly anything so when we went for walks, he'd stop me and ask if he could touch me. At first I didn't like it but he touched my face while I talked. A lot of times he held my hands and he felt my arm muscles once. It was okay, Mom. He wanted to know what I felt like, not just what I sounded like, or smelled like, or acted like.

When he took me fishing at Smithson's Dock, he could check by feel, how I tied the lure on. He could tell what kind fish I had on just by the pull. He could take the fish off the hook for me. When a duck splashed in nearby, Grandpa would ask me what color, then tell me the kind of duck it was."

Mom started to talk and I held my hand up.

"One day I lost my lure to a snag and I thought my day was over, but Grandpa said 'No. Reach into my tacklebox there and hand me the little scratched lure. It's green and white.' I did, and without seeing it he expertly tied it on my line. A minute later I had my best bluegill ever! And Grandpa touched my face and held my shoulders, just to know my joy. It was cool."

Mom interrupted, *"I don't get the point son. We have to go back into the room. I saw Aunt Mary arrive."*

"Please Mom," I said, holding her to her chair. I created some more tears.

"You see, he touched me because that's part of how he knew me. Now, I want to touch him as my goodbye. I gotta do this, Mom."

She looked at me, this time with some attention. "*I get it now*," she said. *"I'm sorry. I'm so caught up in this. Understand that he was your grandpa but he was my Dad too."* She put a Kleenex to her eye.

She looked at me closely for a minute. *"Let's go back in there and you can go back to the casket."*

We did that, and I touched Grandpa's face and his hands. Mom and Dad knelt down next to me.

And she touched him too. For quite a while. And I took the old lure from my pocket and put it next to his hands.

A bit later my sister hissed to me, *"Why did you put that ugly fishing thing on his hands?"*

And I gave her a pissy look and said, *"That's for me to know and you to find out."*

And the organ played.

Proof The Sun Has Moons by George Wylie

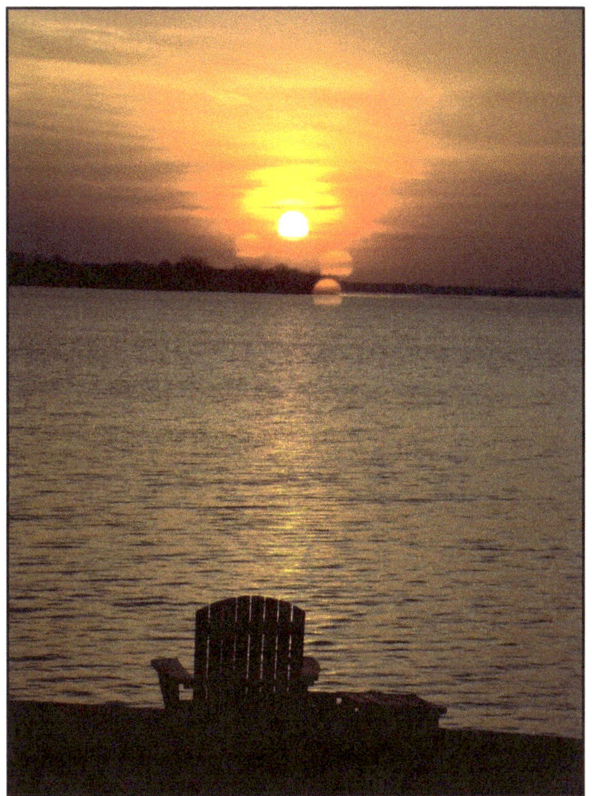

White Raven by John Caviness

As foretold the day would come
the rise of the powerful and foul
high in the sky all would see
above the carnage and violence below;

the spanned wings of a white Raven
their eyes flashed with the sun's rays
cavorting and brandished
images of their fates;

Their gazes returned.
They looked around and saw each other
and put down their weapons.

A Key Wrapped up in a Mystery Inside a Nash Rambler by Bonita Cox Searle

My grandparents related to each other in mysterious ways. As a sixth grader with limited life experience, I found their interactions puzzling, and I tried to make sense of them for future reference and self-protection. Take the day of the Nash Rambler, a key, and the question I finally worked up the nerve to ask.

I was playing hopscotch in the driveway when Grandpa drove up in a brand-new cream and beige 1961 Chevy Impala SS. He patted me on the head and swaggered into the house like he was Dean Martin.

Half an hour later Grandma erupted out the front door, handbag flapping on one arm and a picnic basket under the other. "Bonnie Sue, get in the Rambler. We're driving to Columbus." Columbus! An hour north of Chillicothe! I was about to have An Adventure!

Problem was, she had never driven the car before. Grandpa drove it to his job at the paper mill while she used the go-to-church car for her errands, a car with no pesky clutch to synchronize with the gas pedal.

We jerked out of the driveway.

"Did…Grandpa…buy…a…new…car?" I asked as the car bucked.

"Yes…and…he…won't…let…me…have a…key!"

The Rambler reached a gear it liked and settled down. Grandma's anger, however, bounced around the inside of the car like an errant ping pong ball.

"Who does he think he is, not giving me a key. I didn't know he was even thinking of buying a new car. How am I supposed to go anywhere when he's at work? I'm going to the Chevy dealership in Columbus and demand a key."

Grandpa's many failings were once again brought out for review. I'd heard it all before. My stomach growled, and I wondered what might be in that picnic basket.

When we finally arrived in Columbus, the Chevy dealer was as recalcitrant as Grandpa.

We left with no key.

As she pulled the Rambler onto U.S. 23 for the drive back home, Grandma handed out snacks from the picnic basket. Confident now in her ability to control the car, she steered with one hand while she ate a banana and continued to provide example after example of the poor treatment she had suffered from Grandpa's behavior for the last forty-three years.

I stared out the car window at construction barrels on the edge of the road. The black smudge pots perched on top looked like Wile E. Coyote cartoon bombs. My mind drifted to something I had been pondering since my dad gave me "the talk." The time seemed right to bring it up.

"Grandma, if you hate Grandpa so much, how did you have three children?"

The banana in her hand popped out of its skin and rolled under the gas pedal. The car swerved, knocking over barrels and tossing smudge pots into the ditch. Grandma pulled to the side of the road. She righted the barrels and placed each pot back into position. After she wiped the banana glops off the floor and restarted the Rambler, we juddered back onto the highway.

"Sometimes… these … things… happen," she said.

I couldn't tell if she was deflecting my question or making allowances for her driving.

Either way, she didn't say much the rest of the way home. Her face, however, turned an interesting shade of pink.

We pulled into the driveway, and Grandma stormed into the house. I stayed outside until she yelled through the screen door that supper was ready. It was a quiet meal, and everyone went to bed early.

The next morning Grandpa drove off in the Rambler to work, and

Grandma drove the Chevy Impala to Kroger.

Some mysteries are never solved.

Creek in the Fall by Andrea Haydon

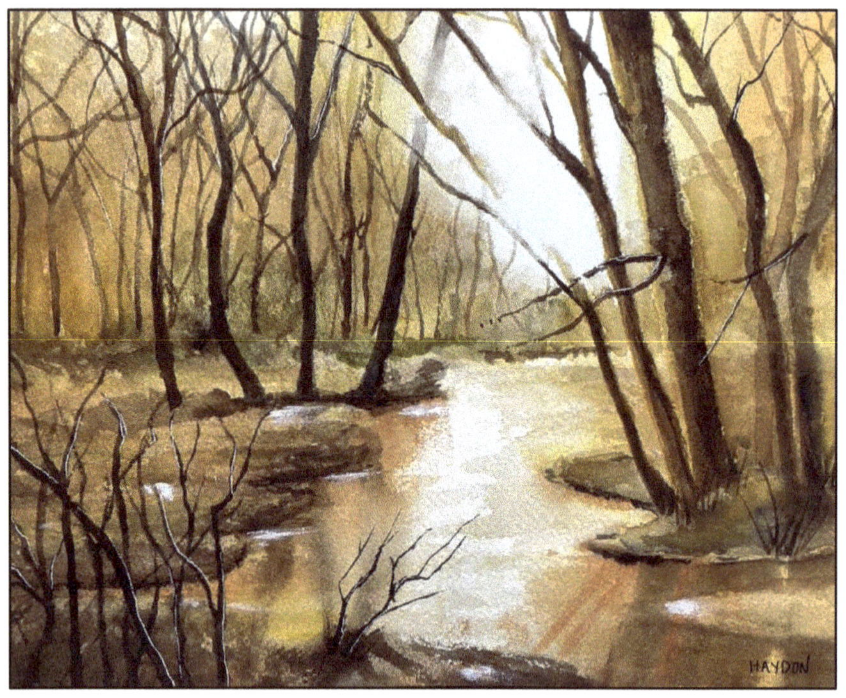

Buried Alive by John Caviness

Warmth between my face and moving pillows
Searching for air as gravity and force push down
Mouth pressed against the glass of their innermost window
Both of us making the sound of a nervous hound

One silently struggling while the other cries in ecstasy
Suffocate me in your thighs he said in one fleeting breath
Entering the brink of one's fantasy
Pleasure mixed with a throttled death

The Family Bungalow by George Wylie

The storm windows needed to be hung each fall, the screens exiled
to the cellar.
It was not an abundant bungalow but an able abode, the lives of five
children etched inside.
Clapboard siding that deserved regular paint yet was rewarded but
a few times
A too-small kitchen that emitted enough sustenance for seven,
and always smelled right.

One bathroom for seven, the tyrant of all the rooms, it dictated
its own order and respect,
Processing its clients just quick enough each school day for
our hygiene and privacy
A small water heater sang which rationed our baths and
our timekeeper mother to guide it
Handmade area rugs dappled the worn creaking floors, protecting
its busy intersections,

A house that rose early and darkened late, it mapped our growth
and nursed us on
Just enough garden for roses and some carrots and a big dependable
rhubarb mound
A box elder we often fell from but provided summer's shade.
A small garage where our heads hit hanging ladders, bikes,
and cobwebs.

A yard that fenced in Tony The Bouncing Dog, who once ate the
neighbor's pet red-tailed hawk
Where Dad poked at dandelions with a hand weeder and hinted
at getting our help
Where robins were so used to children they hopped about us like
traffic cops
Where an overly-dramatic persecuted child could flop onto the grass
in life-ending agony

She was a somewhat demure mother but could make appropriate
declarations when needed.
Her motherly acts were present but only when summoned. She was
the hesitant matron.

Who knew we knew where she put the cookies, her parenting was benign but lasting.
She never loved that house nor bragged about it, but did both those things about her children.

She died peacefully in that house almost forty years ago.
Her progeny are now spread across the world but I've driven by the house a few times.
For me its presence brings no brass fanfare but rather a distant call of *Oh Johnny Boy* or *Taps*.
There are family marks hidden about the place and only we kids know where they are.

I don't have the nerve to ask in and they wouldn't know me. But the house just might.

Heart's Desire by Alys Caviness-Gober

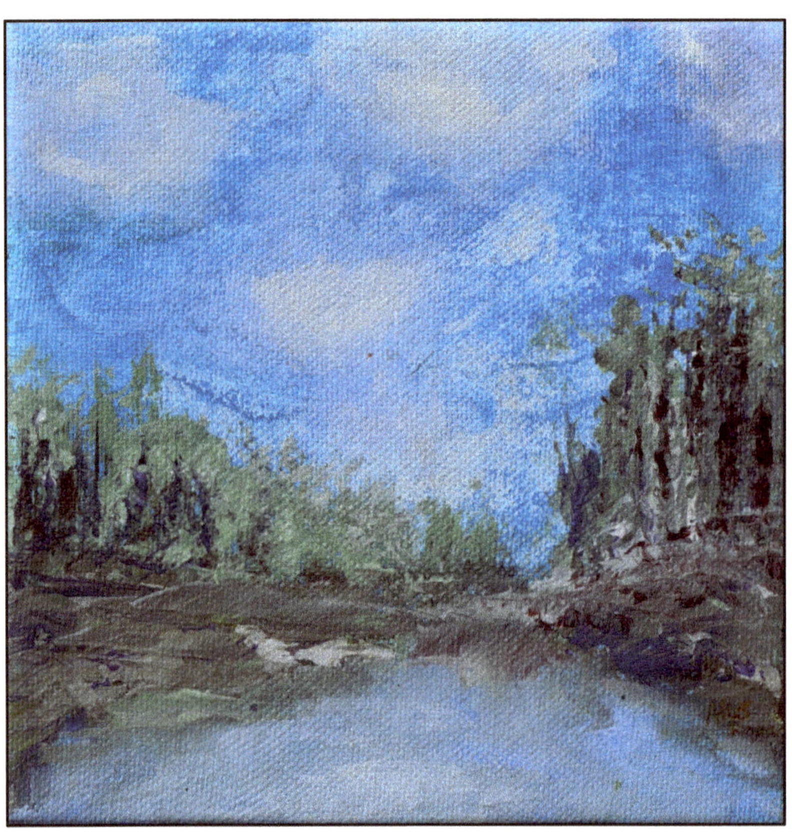

life as an inanimate object by John Caviness

go ahead, pick me up
unleash your hands upon me
interlude our existences and don't let up

take me in your hands, go ahead
allow our sound to fill in what would be
retire me from my soundless dread

go ahead, put me down again
watch as i gather dust and oversee
i'll be waiting until you give in

Untitled 1 by Audrey Barcio

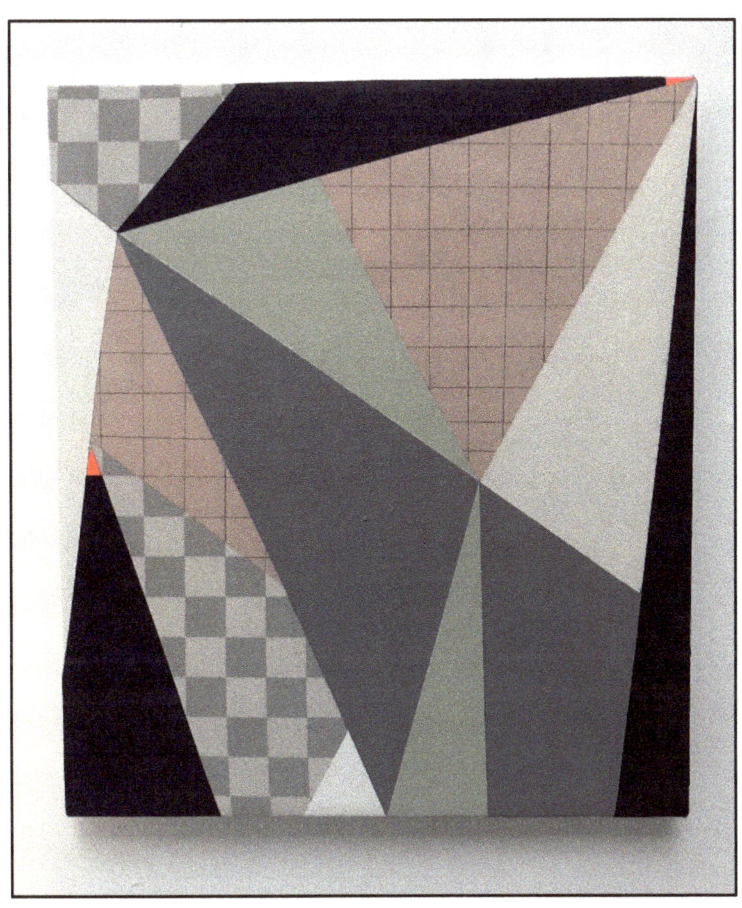

Pork Roast by Deborah J. Petersen

A pork roast in the crockpot
Simmering to its divine,
Your favorite maple glaze
Juicy and sublime.

Rubbed with cumin and ginger
Browned in coconut oil,
Just the way you like it
No matter what the toil.

Favorite side dish yams
And stuffing, oh, so dreamy
Asparagus steamed to perfection,
And gravy thick and creamy.

You loved this dish at ten,
You loved this dish at twenty,
Juicy, juicy pork roast
The memories you bring, a'plenty.

What great kitchen times we had
Years ago when you were younger
Our feasts a hodgepodge of trials
But always squelched our hunger.

We burned some eggs and served fish raw
We didn't add some salt
We were having fun just playing.
It's the wine – and not our fault!

We threw cooked spaghetti on the wall
To see if it was ready
Stick, then yes – fall, then no
Joyful as confetti.

That first apple pie you baked
How exciting, we almost burst.
The lattice work so detailed –
But the dog got there first.

So, here's your magic pot roast

To serve your boyfriend new
Whom we've yet to meet and see –
What? He's vegan? Oh, no! Plan B will have to do!

Walking by Alys Caviness-Gober

She walks alone in the middle of the night, down the middle of roads where the streetlights barely shine. There's no traffic, the streets are empty. The woman has trouble sleeping at night, so she walks. She always has; she always will.

Her walking at night habit is an old one; having worked midnight shifts in her younger years, being out and about in the nighttime feels familiar. She remembers working a 3rd shift fast-food job whilst in college and a 3rd shift production job in her mid-20s. Not a lot of traffic as she'd driven to and from either job. Maybe a long-haul trucker or two passing by, but even in a 24/7 college town, 3rd shift was desolate. In the past there was loneliness walking at night. Now, empty streets feel both familiar and good; in general, empty streets feel relatively good to her. From yards behind her, a lone bicyclist rings his bell, and then rides past, swinging wide around her far to the right, almost to the curb. The bicyclist and the woman both listlessly raise an arm and offer a slight wave in each other's general direction. Obligatory salutation of the sleepless.

Months ago, with the first governmental stay-at-home order, the woman altered her habit and walked in the daytime. She walked on sidewalks or, whenever the sidewalks ended, alongside the curbs of the empty streets. Daytime walks promised other walkers or bicyclists. Bicyclists zoomed past in pairs or small groups, gallantly waving or chin-nodding at walkers and other cyclists. The woman always moved away from everybody else, crossing the street, going into people's yards, and she wore a mask. She could hear some of the walkers scoffing after she'd passed them: *she's sure paranoid!* and *that looks SO ridiculous*; *can you imagine?!*

At first, the maskless daytime walkers walked in pairs or small groups and smiled and waved at other pairs and small groups (and maskless solo walkers), all happily united in a *we got this* attitude, determined *to keep on keeping on*. They chatted amongst themselves; some said encouraging *hellos* and *hang in theres* to passing groups.

Then, the daytime walkers walked in triangular or square formations, one or two on each side of the street, one or two in the middle (forward and rear of the side walkers). They barely spoke to each other.

The nationwide numbers kept rising, both the infected and the dead. As individual state and county and city numbers doubled and then tripled every couple of days, even the scoffers started to see the risks of "normal" behavior, especially regarding physical interactions.

With grim faces, the daytime walkers' heads then bobbed in cursory greeting at triangles and squares of oncoming walkers, all moving as packs to avoid proximity to each other's groups.

One group of triangular or squared walkers would move off into the nearest front yard, maintaining formation as they waited for the other group to pass by on the street. There was no *we got this* camaraderie; silently, *Get the fuck AWAY* hung heavy in the air.

Soon the daytime walkers all wore masks, and they stopped talking, even within their own group. Finally, they all walked alone, not looking up at all except to give a *Get the fuck AWAY* glare from above their masks and to move away from other daytime walkers, who were emitting the same glare from above their own masks.

The daytime bicyclists also stopped riding in pairs and small groups. No more gallant waves, no more lifted chins in silent greetings of solidarity. They rode alone, some zooming as if training for a race (or trying to outrun the devil), some meandering slowly as if hoping that by the time *this* ride ended, things would be back to normal.

The woman stopped being a daytime walker early on, during the scoffing-from-others period: she'd felt then that it was hard enough to keep your metaphorical chin up without being subjected to the ignorance or stupidity of others. When she saw through her front windows the daytime walkers/bicyclists evolve to walking/riding in triangles and squares and wearing masks and then further evolve to walking/riding alone, she still chose nighttime. It was just easier, and with no *Get the fuck AWAY* glares, it was just . . . nicer. Plus, she couldn't sleep at night. Dozing off in the daytime became routine, and unavoidable. She wasn't sure exactly why, but she'd discovered that she could fall asleep for at least 20 minutes at almost any time during the day. There was no good reason not to: it didn't matter what day or what time it was, at least for most people.

Some people were lucky enough to still have jobs: either they were deemed essential and had to go to work (masked, gloved, terrified, angry), or they worked from home. Most of the work-at-homes initially tried to keep up a normal daytime schedule, but a lot of them quickly realized that they could do their work any time, day or night. For those whose jobs had disappeared, unemployment checks were automatically deposited into bank accounts. Infrequent grocery store runs were made during restricted store hours; people stood in line, waiting for their turn to go into the store. Some people wore masks, and some also wore gloves. Millions refused to wear masks or gloves or practice social distancing. They bought into the lies told by the President and his cronies, who chose to ignore science and instead politicized the virus and mask-wearing as anti-freedom and unpatriotic, causing chaos and fear to reign in America for the first year of the pandemic.

One thing was clear: everything that was "normal" before the pandemic might not even exist after it. Other countries, ones with leaders that took the pandemic seriously, fared much better and their citizens were able to get back to something like "normal" after just a few months. At least now, almost a year into the pandemic, with a newly elected administration coming, there's hope, despite the fact that millions of Americans still choose to believe lies told by a President who refuses to even concede he lost the election.

So many people are confused, afraid, and unsure of what's to come. The future feels completely unpredictable, but the woman walks at night in relative peace. She did her duty and voted blue for America to *build back better*. She's content to let her mind wander as her feet take her along her familiar route. Before the pandemic, she regularly changed her nighttime walking routes. Women learned things like that at a young age, because of sexual predators. Who would've imagined that there'd come a day when sexual predators stayed home; even to them, nothing was worth the risk of this particular contagion.

That fact comforts her now, like a familiar tune playing way-in-the-background of her thoughts; *gentle on my mind*, she thinks. She knows that'll probably change after the vaccines, after 70% of the population develops immunity. Then, the streets at night again won't be as empty, won't feel as safe. That thought is a bit troubling, but . . . perhaps people will also build back better, within themselves. Perhaps treating each other better will be the new normal when all this is over.

She walks, and her thoughts move on.

Untitled by Vivianne Belle

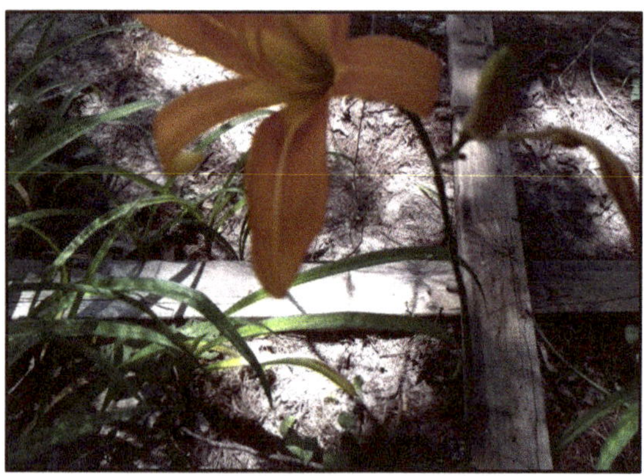

Healing Mountain by John Caviness

Height of the landscape, looming,
driving liquid life down the slopes,
brittle branches in cold wind, vibrating
sauntering beings tread around the oaks.

Poisoned lands lay below, rotting,
taking life and creating resources,
burning branches in blackened piles, heating,
consuming all in sight, through greedy forces.

Beyond the steel of man, towering.
preserving what a creator intended,
unbroken by winds and preying,
living goes on uninterrupted.

Dreamscape 7 by Alys Caviness-Gober

To signal the end of the 2021 published pieces section of this book, here's a little whimsy for you.

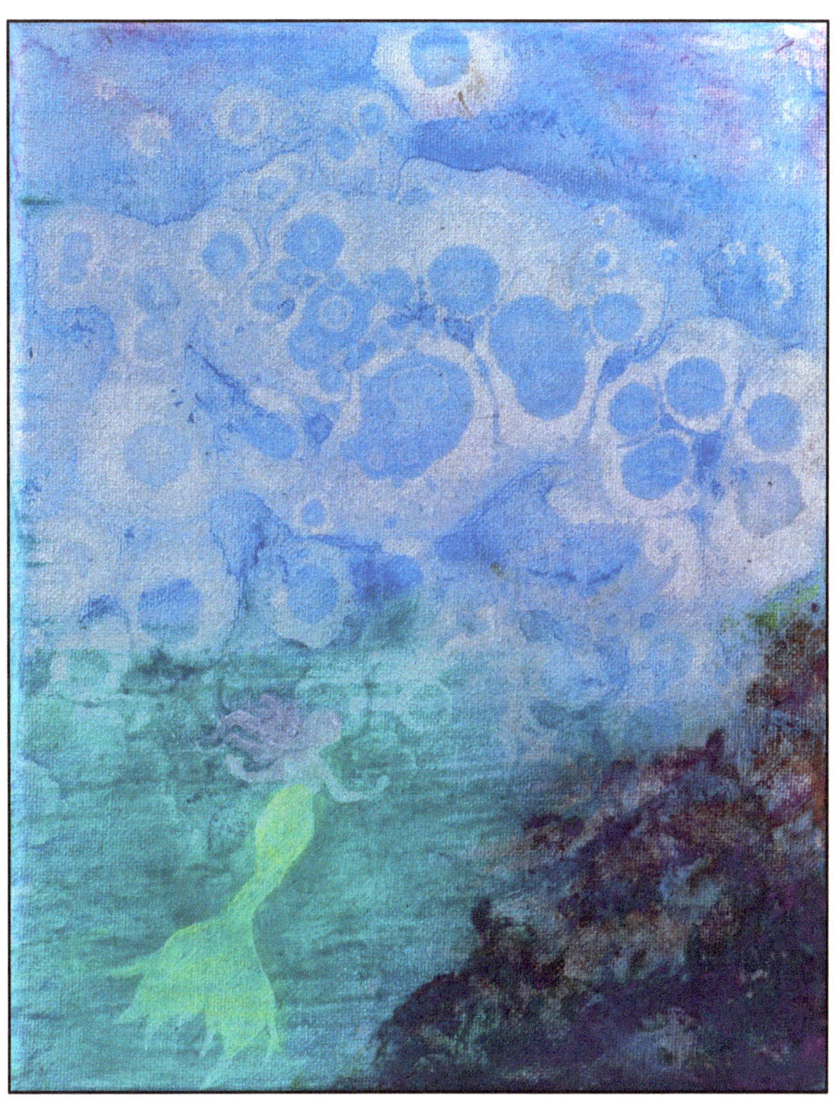

The Polk Street Review Awards

2021 Theme Contest winner: Vivianne Belle

2021 Award of Merit (Best in Book): *Ode to the Comet NEOWISE* by George W. Wolfe

2021 Prose Category:

First Prize: *Rites of Passage* by Patrick Kalahar

Second Prize: *Kitchen Table* by Deborah Petersen

Third Prize: *Traditions passed down from a galaxy far, far away...* by Leah Leach

Honorable Mention: *A Key Wrapped up in a Mystery Inside a Nash Rambler* by Bonita Cox Searle

2021 Poetry/Song Lyrics Category:

First Prize: *Thanksgiving Ghosts* by Bonita Cox Searle

Second Prize: *The Crepe Myrtle* by Michael J. Strosahl

Third Prize: *The Loneliness of His Discontent* by George Wylie

Honorable Mention: *Caretaker's Melody* by Jenny Kalahar

2021 Images Category:

First Prize: *Man on pier* by George Wylie

Second Prize: *Untitled 2* by Audrey Barcio

Third Prize: *Alcohol Ink Mugs* by Andrea Haydon
(Andrea made the mugs and took the great photograph of them)

2021 Special Awards:

Special Award: E. A. Wasonga

E. A. (Emily) Wasonga is the owner of *@LHOCreations*, and we present a *Special Award* to her for consistently submitting thought-provoking and beautifully written pieces to this publication over the many years of its existence, and for her dedication to fundraising for *CEArts* and our *TPSR* books.

Special Award: Kim Carlson

Kim is new to *The Polk Street Review*, and her first-ever submission to this publication shares elements of her journey of healing as an abuse survivor. For her bravery in publicly sharing her story, we present Kim with a *Special Award.*

Contributor Biographies

Audrey Barcio is an artist living in Chicago, IL. She's an Assistant Professor at Ball State University in Muncie, IN (she commutes!). Her work negates the heritage of abstraction intersecting with the tools of the virtual industrial age. Using universal symbology rooted in the language of early abstractionists, her work strives to transcend the accepted cultural *raison d'être*. Barcio received her BAE from Herron School of Art and Design and her MFA from the University of Nevada, Las Vegas. She attended the Pont-Aven School of Contemporary Art in Brittany, France, and completed a Vermont Studio Center residency in 2017, and is a 2019 Pollock - Krasner Foundation Grant recipient. Her work has been published in New American Paintings and has been featured in multiple group exhibitions around the U.S., including Art in America at the Art Miami Satellite Fair, ART IN CONTEXT: Selections from the Marjorie Barrick Museum of Art Collection, Las Vegas, NV, and GLAMFA at UC Long Beach. Recent solo exhibitions include Syracuse University, New York, the Las Vegas Government Center, Las Vegas, NV, University of Nevada, Las Vegas, and Tube Factory, Indianapolis, IN. Barcio's work is included in several public and private collections, including that of the Barrick Museum of Art. More about Audrey: http://audreybarcio.com.

Vivianne Belle lives in Noblesville. She enjoys traveling abroad and occasionally putting pen to paper to write poetry and prose.

Kim Carlson is an outsider artist. Outsider art is derived from individuals with little to no formal art instruction or knowledge; outside art is a gnostic art form. The term *gnosis* refers to something that is 'known' directly from the source of all that is and tends to have mystical qualities about it. Outsider artists are often marginalized in Western society, misunderstood, misrepresented, and misinterpreted in and among the cultures, communities, and families, making many of them labeled as mentally ill and/or disabled. For Kim, being an outsider artist means that her spirit and intuition guide what she creates. Kim's art has evolved through anime and comic book-style art to painting, mixed media, dance, written word, teaching, nursing, coaching, and Tarot card readings and interpretations. Kim believes the ultimate mission of the outsider artist is to awaken in themselves their authenticity, transform the world they see around them from pain and suffering to joy, love, and inspiration, and then to go out into the world and shine with hope and light to inspire others to do the same. Follow Kim on Instagram at kim.carlson.art.

John Caviness grew up in Noblesville, graduating from Noblesville High School, and received a Bachelor of Arts in Foreign Languages (German Studies) and Master of Science from the *Center for Communication and Information Sciences* (CICS) at Ball State University. John loves to fix problems, ease frustration, and optimize quality of life while working with technology, and he helps the company he works for and their clients thrive in the modern technological landscape. John troubleshoots technology problems large and small in industry spaces like healthcare, construction, storage, security, paper, government, machinery, food, landscaping, real estate, religious organizations, and research companies. John has been a male ally to women throughout his life and hopes he can help both men and women work together better in the technology space. You can find out about John's wood-carving artistry here: https://www.holzcave.com/.

Alys Caviness-Gober is an anthropologist, artist, and writer. Despite lifelong disabilities, she perseveres with her art and nonprofit volunteering. Alys taught Anthropology, Women's Studies, and ESOL at the university level, and was a PhD candidate in Applied

Linguistics until her disabilities worsened in 2009. In 2011, Alys began selling artwork (*Creative Expressions Arts*). She is juried into the *Hamilton County Artists' Association* in both photography and 2D categories. Alys and author Sarah E. Morin are the cofounders of the literature-based annual project *Noblesville Interdisciplinary Creativity Expo* (NICE). In November 2014, Alys founded *Logan Street Sanctuary, Inc.* (LSS), an all-volunteer 501(c)(3) Arts organization; in July 2019, LSS rebranded as *Community • Education • Arts* (CEArts). Alys serves as the President of *CEArts*, and Sarah E. serves as the Secretary. Under their leadership, in late 2019 *CEArts* expanded with digital content, including online *Arts Showcase* exhibit opportunities for writers, musicians, and artists, and @theroundtable, an arts-related podcast/short videos series. Alys is a FY2017 (July 2016 - June 2017) Indiana Arts Commission *Individual Artist Project* Grant Award recipient, creating a series of large-scale paintings expressing life with hidden disabilities. She was selected to participate in the IUPUI Arts and Humanities Institute's *Religion Spirituality, and the Arts* 2018/19 Seminar Class, and has been an invited presenter at *Poetry Society of Indiana* conferences (2017, 2018, 2019). Alys is a selected poet for *INverse: Indiana's Poetry Archive*, and is a member of *Noble Poets* and the *Poetry Society of Indiana*. Her poetry has been featured in global anthologies since the 1980s, and in her own poetry and artwork collections, *Naked In Wonderland (Volumes I, II,* and *III*). She serves on the *Noblesville Cultural Arts Council* and is active in the local arts scene. Alys' artwork, photographs, and poetry have received national and international recognition.

Lori Cates Hand is Executive Editor for DK Publishing, where she manages English-language adaptations of its lifestyle, reference, travel, children's, and licensed books. She and her husband, Jason, have lived in Noblesville for more than 20 years and have a teenage daughter. Lori volunteers extensively in the community, including as Secretary of the NHS Choir Parent Organization and a founding member of the Noblesville Democratic Club. She has a BA in English Literature from the University of Evansville and studied at Harlaxton College in Grantham, England.

Andrea Haydon is the proprietor of ***Studio Haydon LLC***, a multifaceted art and design firm in Indianapolis. Andrea has been studying and creating art for nearly 30 years. She has studied experiential art and design in Hesse, Germany, was a part of the design team that created the graphics for Super Bowl XLVI in Indianapolis, has served as an adjunct professor at Herron School of Art + Design, and was named one of the Top 100 Best Young Advertisers in the Country by the Art Directors Club of New York. Andrea lives in Garfield Park, where you'll find her enjoying a pint at Garfield Brewery, playing her violin, practicing yoga, painting, or hanging out with her cat/roommate Karl. For more about Andrea and her artwork, go to http://www.studiohaydon.com/.

Jenny Kalahar is the author of ten books and has been published in several anthologies, in literary journals, and in her humor column in *Tails Magazine*. She and husband Patrick previously owned and operated bookshops in Michigan and Ohio, and now sell books via the internet. They are active in the poetry community of Indiana, and Jenny is the publisher of the *Poetry Society of Indiana*, the founder and leader of *Last Stanza Poetry Association*, and the president of the *Youth Poetry Society of Indiana*. She was nominated for the Indiana state Poet Laureate position and twice nominated for a Pushcart Prize in poetry. When not writing, reading, or working with old books, she loves expeditions through flea markets and playing piano and percussion.

Patrick Kalahar is a used and rare bookseller with his wife, Jenny, and a book conservationist in Elwood, Indiana. He is a veteran, world traveler, avid reader, and book collector. He was one of the main interviewees in the Emmy Award-winning documentary, *James Whitcomb Riley, Hoosier Poet.* He is a member of Last Stanza Poetry Association, and his poems have been published in *Tipton Poetry Journal, Flying Island, Last Stanza Poetry Journal,* and the anthologies: *The Moon and Humans, Rail Lines,* and *A Disconsolate Planet.*

Chuck Kellum grew up on a farm southwest of Indianapolis. As a young adult he traveled the world a bit – about twenty countries in all. He settled into a technology-related career primarily as a business applications software developer, got and stayed married, helped raise three children, and has lived in Anderson since 1984. He began writing poetry while a senior in college studying engineering. Chuck wrote about 120 poems in the course of a dozen years before getting married, but then was too busy with work and family. His writing of poems on a somewhat frequent basis resumed in 2009 after he was no longer working full time. He's been a member of the *Noble Poets* club since 2017, and currently serves as Treasurer of the *Poetry Society of Indiana*.

Dr. Leah Leach is a Noblesville resident and the founder of the *Gal's Guide Library* (located in Nickel Plate Arts' campus in Noblesville) – home to the first women's history lending-library in the United States. She is a highly sought-after educator. Leah's programs incorporate history and movies with big energy, interaction, and personability. Winner of 5 podcast awards and 12 film awards, Leah's background is in film and podcast production.

Marlene Million is a member of Noble Poets, Poetry Society of Indiana, and National Fed. of State Poetry Societies, Inc. She has been published in The Polk Street Review, Tipton Poetry Journal, Ink to Paper, Poetry and Paint, several book and anthologies. She has recently published a poetry chapbook entitled: In Light of Joy.

Sarah E. Morin serves as a kidwrangler at Conner Prairie, a history museum in Fishers, Indiana. She writes and performs unruly fairy tales and poems and is a regular performer at Fairyville at Nickel Plate Arts. She has published two books, *Waking Beauty (*a Christian fantasy novel based on Sleeping Beauty) and *Rapunzel the Hairbrained,* a children's picture book that forms the basis of a workshop to build girls' self-esteem. Sarah E. is the Premier Poet of *Poetry Society of Indiana*, Secretary of *Community • Education • Arts*, and co-founder of *NICE* (Noblesville Interdisciplinary Creativity Expo). She loved the years she spent living above the Clock Shop in Noblesville, and still remains engaged in the downtown scene through *Noble Poets* (new poets welcome – 3rd Tuesday each month at 6:30PM in Zoom during the pandemic). When she grows up, she wants to be a child prodigy. Visit her at sarahemorin.com.

Sandra Nantais is a poet, essayist, and photographer who relocated from Northwest Indiana to the Piney Woods of Northern Louisiana in 2016. She captures the dusty history of the many abandoned properties of her new surroundings pulling new stories with the old.

Michelle "Meesh" Payne lives in Noblesville, only three blocks from the iconic Town Square. She works full-time as AVP of Branding & Communications in Downtown Indy at Elements

Financial, one of the area's largest credit unions. Michelle has been there for 17 years. Besides spending a lot of time working and commuting, she is raising two daughters, ages 15 & 10, and two pups, ages 7 and 9 months. Please visit her blog at www.iamnotyourmom.com for more of her essays about life as a middle-aged professional with a family and many other interests and roles and deep thoughts.

Deborah Petersen is an educator, and for decades she taught middle and high school students and was a Composition professor at some local colleges as well. She is the current President of the *Poetry Society of Indiana*, as well as a Poetry Contest judge for national and state contests. Deborah has been the editor and contributor to three poetry anthologies and was a featured poet in the *Indiana Voice Journal*. It is no secret to anyone who knows Deborah that she is the living epitome of "a Word Junkie." What first influenced Deborah as a poet were the prayers of her childhood. Later, she was influenced by the complexity and cadence of William Shakespeare's works. The most recent years have moved her with the writings of the Persian Poet and Sufi Mystic, Rumi, and by the Japanese Haiku Master, Basho. As artists, Deborah believes we are mere conduits. When she is in the moment of being a conduit, she finds herself in an omniscience, a moment of vastness and grace, a connection to a universal wisdom and discerning perception.

Noah R. attends Noblesville East Middle School and likes playing with his friends.

Bonita Cox Searle is an Indiana native, poet, and writer who has lived in Noblesville for over 20 years. Her work has appeared in *Flying Island, Indiana Voice Journal*, *The Polk Street Review*, and *The Last Stanza Journal*.

Ndaba Sibanda is a 2019 Pushcart Prize nominee, who's poems have been widely anthologized. His work is featured in *The Anthology House,* in *The New Shoots Anthology*, and in *The Van Gogh Anthology*, and A *Worldwide Anthology of One Hundred Poetic Intersections*. Ndaba's works are in *Page & Spine, Peeking Cat, Piker Press, SCARLET LEAF REVIEW, Universidad Complutense de Madrid, the Pangolin Review, Kalahari Review, Botsotso, The Ofi Press Magazine, Hawaii Pacific Review, Deltona Howl, The song is,*

Indian Review, Eunoia Review, JONAH magazine, Saraba Magazine, Poetry Potion, Saraba Magazine, The Borfski Press, Snippets, East Coast Literary Review, Random Poem Tree, festival-of-language, and *Whispering Prairie Press.* Sibanda's book *Notes, Themes, Things And Other Things: Confronting Controversies, Contradictions And Indoctrinations* was considered for The 2019 Restless Book Prize for New Immigrant Writing in Nonfiction. Ndaba's book *Cabinet Meetings: Of Big And Small Preys* was considered for The Graywolf Press Africa Prize 2018. Sibanda's books include *Timbomb*, *Dear Dawn And Daylight*, *Sometimes Seasons Come With Unseasonal Harvests*, *A Different Ballgame* and *The Way Forward.* Ndaba Sibanda is the author of *The Gushungo Way*, *Sleeping Rivers*, *Love O'Clock, The Dead Must Be Sobbing, Football of Fools, Cutting-edge Cache: Unsympathetic Untruth, Of the Saliva and the Tongue, When Inspiration Sings In Silence*, and *Poetry Pharmacy.* Ndaba blogs here*: Let's Get Cracking! – Ndaba Sibanda.*

Warren Sidwell has lived in central Indiana his entire life, calling Noblesville home for the past 20 years. Warren's wife and daughters are the reasons he gets out of bed each day and playing with his dogs keeps him out of bed. Writing is a passion that Warren hasn't given proper fuel to in many years.

Michael E. Strosahl is originally from Moline, Illinois. After moving to Indiana, he became very active in the poetry community. His work has been seen before in *The Polk Street Review*, also in the *Tipton Poetry Journal*, *Last Stanza Journal*, *Bards Against Hunger*, and online at *Medusa's Kitchen*, *Indiana Voice Journal*, *Project Agent Orange*, and *Our Day's Encounter*. He has relocated to Jefferson City, Missouri where he co-hosts a critiquing group in the capital city and appears weekly at the literary site Moristotle & Company.

Steve VandeWater has resided in Noblesville for 30 years, where he and his wife Brenda have raised three children. A decorative concrete contractor by trade, Steve has only recently begun writing and performing songs as a creative outlet. Steve's lyrics, poetry and short stories have appeared in editions of *The Polk Street Review* since 2017.

E. A. Wasonga is a social entrepreneur and philanthropist. Visit the organization she founded: www.LHoCreations.world.

George W. Wolfe is Professor Emeritus and former Director of the Ball State University *Peace and Conflict Studies*. He is the author of over 50 articles on the website *Voices of Humanity*, and three books, including his latest collection of poetry entitled: *Clapping with One Hand: Poems Inspired by Zen, Mozart and my Experience of India*. His first book, *The Spiritual Power of Nonviolence: Interfaith Understanding for a Future Without War* has been endorsed by Arun Gandhi and by Judy O'Bannon, the former First Lady of Indiana. Wolfe is also an accomplished classical saxophonist who has appeared as a soloist with the Royal Band of the Belgian Air Force, the United States Navy Band, the Saskatoon Symphony, the Chautauqua Motet Choir, the Indianapolis Children's Choir, and the Indianapolis Symphonic Band.

George Wylie has only been writing poetry for four years but he is quite active, with a book, *Why Did I Remain In The Garden*, some contests, and online venues such as World Poetry Open Mic, Speakeasy Cafe, Allpoetry.com, and others. He is co-leader of the Downriver Poets & Playwrights, and runs a Facebook poetry page: *George Wylie Writes*.

About Community Education Arts

Community • Education • Arts, Inc. (CEArts) is a 501(c)(3) nonprofit Arts organization that is based in Noblesville with a global reach. Our organization is run by a small band of dedicated people volunteering time out of their busy lives to keep our nonprofit alive.

The Things We Love To Do

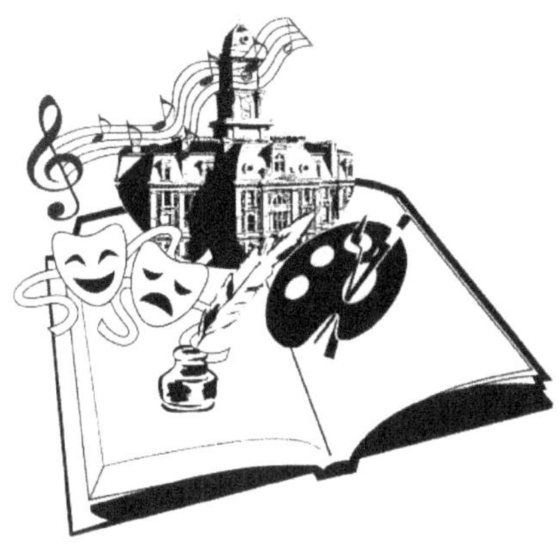

We will continue to meet COVID-19's challenges head-on, using Zoom for workshops and recording @theroundtable podcast episodes featuring artists interviews and behind-the-scenes discussions for our annual *NICE* (Noblesville Interdisciplinary Creativity Expo) project, and hosting online Arts Showcase exhibits on our website. This year's *The Polk Street Review* (TPSR) book launch is a virtual event as well.

A special *thank you* to our 2021 volunteers for all their hard work!

2021 CEArts Volunteers

Board Officers:
President: Alys Caviness-Gober
Secretary: Sarah E. Morin
Treasurer: Joyce Perry

CEArts Irregulars (our intrepid volunteers):
Cris Gober
James Weston

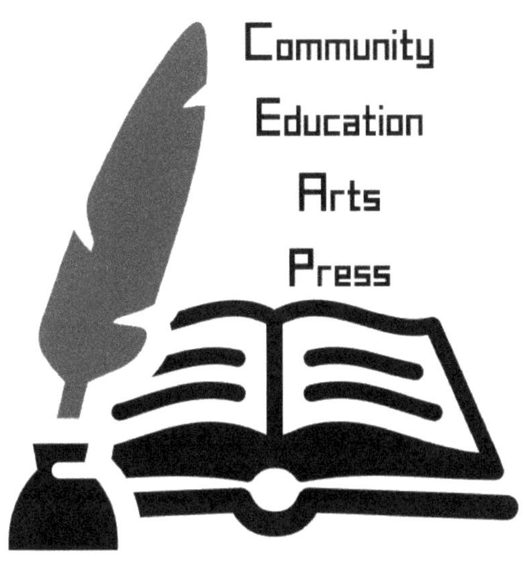

The Polk Street Review is published by
Community • Education • Arts Press
a division of
Community • Education • Arts, Inc.
Noblesville, IN 46060
CEArts.org
info@cearts.org

www.ingramcontent.com/pod-product-compliance
Lightning Source LLC
LaVergne TN
LVHW052347100826
845147LV00012B/768

* 9 7 8 0 9 9 9 8 8 5 8 6 4 *